GUIDE TO THE
Gardens
OF
Georgia

LILLY PINKAS

PHOTOGRAPHS BY JOSEPH PINKAS

Line illustrations by Frank Lohan

PINEAPPLE PRESS, INC.

SARASOTA, FLORIDA

Inquiries should be addressed to:

Pineapple Press, Inc.
P.O. Box 3899
Sarasota, Florida 34230
www.pineapplepress.com.

Library of Congress Cataloging in Publication Data

Pinkas, Lilly.
        Guide to the gardens of Georgia / Lilly Pinkas ; photographs by
Joseph Pinkas.— 1st ed.
                p.   cm.
        ISBN 1-56164-198-7 (alk. paper)
1. Gardens—Georgia—Guidebooks. 2. Georgia—Guidebooks. I. Pinkas,
Joseph. II. Title.

SB466.U65 G47 2000
712'.09758—dc21   99-053479

                                        CIP

First Edition
10 9 8 7 6 5 4 3 2 1

Design by Osprey Design Systems, Bradenton, Florida
Typesetting by Sandra Wright's Designs, Sanford, Florida
Printed and bound by Versa Press, Inc., East Peoria, Illinois

Acknowledgments

I would like to express my sincere thanks to Dr. Brinsley Burbidge, executive director of Denver Botanic Garden, for his respected advice and for his time in reviewing the manuscript. A very special thanks to Alston Glenn, executive director of Atlanta Botanical Garden, and Mildred Pinnell, horticulturist at Atlanta Botanical Garden, for their expertise and help in reviewing the manuscript. Many thanks to Barry I. Smith and Eugenia H. Lehmann of Augusta, Georgia, for their advice about historical facts concerning Augusta and Pendleton King Park. And the biggest thanks goes to Lenka Wagner for editing the first drafts of the manuscript, a truly Herculean task.

Lookout
Mountain ■

Hiawassee ■

Dahlonega
■

Highlands

Adairsville
■ ■
Mount
Berry

Athens
■

Loganville ■
☆ ■
Decatur

Atlanta

Piedmont

Augusta
■

Georgia

Pine Mountain
■

Macon
●

Milledgeville
■

Fort Valley ■

● Columbus

Statesboro ■
Metter ■

Savannah ■

Plains

Coastal

Thomasville ■ ■
Valdosta

Table of Contents

continued

Table of Contents, *continued*

Preface

Doctors Lilly and Joseph Pinkas were introduced to me as "two remarkable people who have produced an excellent book titled *Guide to the Gardens of Florida*." Their second book is a result of their visits to gardens in Georgia and is also excellent.

There are many wonderful and varied gardens within the state of Georgia. Looking over the *Guide to the Gardens of Georgia* table of contents, the two characteristics I find in common to all thirty-two gardens described is their uniqueness and the fact that each is open to public viewing. It is helpful that these gardens have been grouped geographically from the Coastal and Plains Regions of the south through the Piedmont and up to the Highlands Region in the northernmost area of Georgia. This geographical organization becomes a highly useful aid when focusing on plants that live in similar habitats and also a convenience with regard to travel. The information contained in *Guide to the Gardens of Georgia* will be of great interest and practical value to both residents and visitors to our state. Whether you are an active gardener, researcher, or someone who enjoys looking at gardens from the perspective of their contribution to the visual arts, I commend this book as a faithful resource and travel companion.

Alston Glenn
Executive Director
Atlanta Botanical Garden

Foreword

The gardens of Georgia are, with every justification, of national importance and stature. They are also imperfectly known and there has long been a need for this publication, which creates the desire to make a visit and also provides all of the information to simplify the process. Joseph and Lilly Pinkas have opened the door to a whole world of garden discovery in this beautiful state.

I read the draft text for this book with a feeling of growing excitement about the gardens of Georgia, an excitement generated by the fact that this is no ordinary "formula" travel guide. Lilly Pinkas has visited every garden personally in the last year, and her recommendations are based on her own observations, seen through her eyes as an experienced gardener with an unfailing eye for design and for excellence. In reading the text, I can visualize how the garden looks and even deduce the level of maintenance and what she might say, if asked to comment candidly, about the garden staff. She is a true master of writing for other gardeners and plant enthusiasts.

Lilly's text has the perfect accompaniment in the evocative photographs of Joseph Pinkas. An accomplished photographer, he is also a dedicated and knowledgeable gardener with a great eye for what entices us as fellow gardeners. His pictures add a whole new level of information to the text but do not duplicate it. They provide insight into what makes these gardens great. Text and photographs are a true partnership that mirrors Lilly and Joseph's partnership as gardeners, as enthusiastic communicators about their love for gardens, and as life companions.

I welcome this book as I welcomed their book on the gardens of Florida. It will become a constant traveling companion for Georgia residents and tourists alike, and it will open up new doors. If you love gardens and if you love the state of Georgia, you will love this book.

Dr. Brinsley Burbidge
Executive Director
Denver Botanic Gardens

Introduction

The thirty-two gardens described in this book are certainly a diverse group. They range in size from a city garden on one-eighth acre to a sprawling garden of 2,500 acres. Their origins are as varied as their present resources and their future goals. There are many purposes to these gardens, from display and amusement to education, research, and conservation. But above all, gardens are oases of quiet peace and places of beauty in our hurried, noisy, and increasingly complex world.

We hope that our list of gardens is totally comprehensive. We traveled through Georgia many times in search of gardens, and we firmly believe we found every single one. But if you find one that we missed, please write to us in care of the publisher so we can include it in the next edition. The sixty additional places mentioned are not gardens as such, but we felt they could be of interest to garden, plant, and nature lovers.

We gave a great deal of thought to the planning of our trips but originally we were not quite sure in what order to proceed. Should we go from north to south or from east to west? We decided to start in Savannah because that is where, in February 1733, General James Oglethorpe and his settlers arrived to establish England's thirteenth and last colony. And it was here that an experimental garden was established within one month of the colonists' arrival, making this ten-acre garden the first experimental garden not just in Georgia but in America (not including the agricultural efforts of Native Americans). From the original settlement in Savannah, the colonists proceeded further inland. So there it is—we started in Savannah and then continued inland; it seemed only logical.

We felt that including the proper travel directions certainly makes the trips easier and more enjoyable, and the complete address and phone number for each garden should make it easier to inquire before you go concerning best times to visit, flowering peaks, and any changes in the garden's hours and facilities.

We are sure that during your own travels as you visit the gardens, you will have a great deal of fun and enjoy the beauty of the gardens. We surely did.

Coastal Region

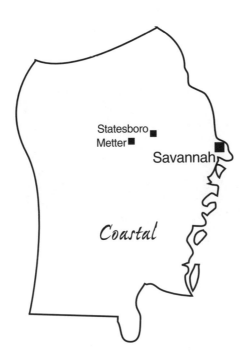

Statesboro ■
Metter ■
Savannah

Coastal

Andrew Low House

A small city garden surrounds this beautiful mansion. The front entry garden is one of only four parterre gardens in Savannah to retain its original design.

Address: 329 Abercorn Street, Savannah, GA 31401

Directions: From I-95 take exit 17 to I-16. Go east on I-16 to the city of Savannah, where I-16 becomes Montgomery Street. Make an immediate right turn onto W. Charlton Street; continue past Pulaski and Madison Squares to Lafayette Square. The house will be on your left, in the SW corner of Lafayette Square.

Hours: 10:30 a.m. to 4:00 p.m. weekdays; 12:00 p.m. to 4:00 p.m. Sundays

Closed: Thursdays and all major holidays

Admission fee: yes

Wheelchair access: gardens, yes; house, no

Facilities: none

Area: 1/4 acre

Phone: (912) 233-6854

Designed by architect John Norris, this beautiful mansion of mid-nineteenth-century design was built in 1848 for Andrew Low, a wealthy cotton merchant. The house reflects a West Indian influence, extensive balconies enclosed by cast-iron railings and shuttered piazzas. William Makepeace Thackeray was a guest in the house in the 1850s, as was General Robert E. Lee in 1870. And in 1912 it was in this house that Juliette Gordon Low organized the first Girl Scout troop in America. The house now is Headquarters of the National Society of the Colonial Dames of America.

The small, symmetrical front entry garden enclosed by a cast-iron fence is one of only four parterre gardens in the city of Savannah to retain its original design. **Azaleas** are planted along the front fence, and hedges of **yew** stretch along the sides. Four **holly trees**, planted in formal symmetry, are skillfully trimmed and shaped.

Brick walls with plantings of **azaleas** alongside surround the back garden. **Sycamore trees** and **magnolias** provide shade, **dogwood trees** show off their beautiful snowy white blossoms, and the heavy fragrance of **confederate jasmine** permeates the air. **Ferns** surround the water fountain on the brick wall, and white **Lady Banksia rose** and **trumpet honeysuckle** climb all over iron railings.

Lady Banksia rose (*Rosa banksiae*), native to China, is a climbing, semi-evergreen, and thornless rose, blooming in late spring. During the massive flowering, one-inch blooms thickly cover the plant lasting for a few weeks. This rose can be found in four main forms—yellow or white, single or double. The yellow, double-flowering, intensely fragrant variety seems to be most popular in Southern gardens. **Trumpet honeysuckle** (*Lonicera sempervirens*) is a native American vine, favored in the South since colonial times. The honeysuckle is attractive to butterflies and hummingbirds and shows off its trumpet-shaped, orange-red clusters of blooms in late spring and early summer.

Worth Seeing: Take the tour of the **Andrew Low House,** painstakingly restored to its 1840 period. See beautiful rooms decorated with plaster cornices, crystal chandeliers, and elaborately carved woodwork. The members and friends of the Society of the Georgia Colonial Dames donated most of the exquisite, museum-quality furnishings in the house.

Isaiah Davenport House Museum

This small, intimate period garden is not original to the house.
It was created in 1976 as a bicentennial project.

Address: 324 E. State Street, Savannah, GA 31401
Directions: From I-95 take exit 17 to I-16. Go east on I-16 to the
    city of Savannah, where I-16 becomes Montgomery Street. Go 0.3
    miles, then make a right turn onto W. Oglethorpe Avenue.
    Continue on Oglethorpe Avenue until Habersham Street, then
    make a left turn towards Columbia Square. House is on the corner
    of Habersham and E. State Streets.
Hours: 10:00 a.m. to 4:30 p.m. daily
Closed: major holidays
Admission fee: museum, yes; garden, no.
Wheelchair access: partial
Facilities: museum shop
Area: 1/8 acre
Phone: (912) 236-8097

This house, started in 1815 and completed in 1820 by Isaiah
Davenport, is an exceptionally fine example of American
Federal–style architecture. Davenport, a Rhode Island master
builder who was trained as a shipwright, came to Savannah in 1807
to participate in the building boom that followed the disastrous fire
of 1796. He prospered as a builder, became a city alderman, and died
during a yellow fever outbreak in 1827. During the 1920s and
1930s, Davenport's house had become a tenement, chopped up into
several small apartments. And in the mid 1950s, the events seemed
to go from bad to worse. Speculators were quite determined to
demolish the house, sell the old bricks, and create yet another
parking lot. When demolition seemed imminent, seven courageous
ladies gathered their determination, vision, and cash to stop it. How
lucky we all are that they managed to stop the demolition. That is
how the Historic Savannah Foundation started, and the Isaiah
Davenport House was restored as its first project. From this beginning, the Historic Savannah Foundation has saved over 1,700 histori-
cally significant properties so far and, without question, remains a

city leader in historic preservation. Isaiah Davenport House was opened to the public as a museum in 1963.

The small period garden is not original to the house. The Savannah Trustees' Garden Club created it in 1976 as a bicentennial project. Further plantings were added in 1996. Enjoy plantings of **azaleas** along brick walls and paths, fragrant white blossoms of a **dogwood** in the spring, clipped **boxwood hedges,** perennials, seasonal annuals as well as a small round reflecting pool.

Juliette Gordon Low Birthplace

This small Victorian parterre garden was designed by well-known landscape architect Clermont Lee.

Address: 142 Bull Street, Savannah, GA 31401

Directions: From I-95 take exit 17 to I-16. Go east on I-16 to the city of Savannah, where I-16 becomes Montgomery Street. Continue on Montgomery Street until you make a right turn onto W. Oglethrope Avenue. Go for four blocks until Bull Street. The house is on the corner of Oglethorpe Avenue and Bull Street.

Hours: 10:00 a.m. to 4:00 p.m. Monday, Tuesday, Thursday, Friday, and Saturday; 12:30 p.m. to 4:30 p.m. Sunday

Closed: Wednesdays, St.Patrick's Day, Christmas Eve, Christmas Day, New Year's Eve, and New Year's Day

Admission fee: yes

Wheelchair access: partial

Facilities: museum shop

Area: 1/8 acre

Phone: (912) 233-4501

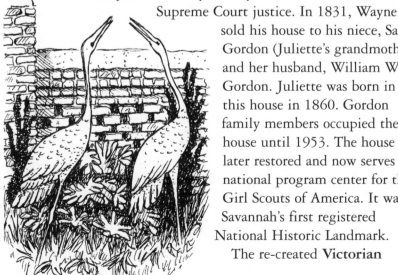

The Wayne-Gordon House, a Regency-style townhouse located in the heart of Savannah's Historic District, was completed in1821 for James M. Wayne, mayor of Savannah and later a Supreme Court justice. In 1831, Wayne sold his house to his niece, Sarah Gordon (Juliette's grandmother), and her husband, William W. Gordon. Juliette was born in this house in 1860. Gordon family members occupied the house until 1953. The house was later restored and now serves as a national program center for the Girl Scouts of America. It was Savannah's first registered National Historic Landmark.

The re-created **Victorian**

Garden was designed by landscape architect Clermont Lee; it is of parterre design, with symmetrical beds and crushed oyster shell paths bordered with bricks. Plantings of **azaleas, camellias, crape myrtles,** and **flowering almonds** are featured, to mention just a few. Vines festoon the wrought-iron fence. During the spring enjoy the fragrances of **wisteria** and **confederate jasmine** that permeate the garden.

Chinese wisteria (*Wisteria sinensis*) is a deciduous vine native to China and is extremely popular throughout the Southeast. Its fragrant clusters of violet-blue flowers, up to a foot in length, are a sight to remember. And the display is even more spectacular because blossoms occur on bare stems before leaves appear. **Confederate jasmine** (*Trachelospermum jasminoides*) is another native of China. This vine is quite popular in Southern gardens and is prized for its fragrant flowers and evergreen foliage. Star-shaped, intensely fragrant white flowers blossom in profusion in late spring and early summer.

The bronze statues of cranes by the entry gate to the garden came as a gift from one of the Chinese Imperial Gardens.

Richardson-Owens-Thomas House

The recreation of this 1820s period garden was designed by landscape architect Clermont Lee. This small, formal, and symmetrical English Regency garden is surrounded by walls of tabby and brick.

Address: 124 Abercorn Street, Savannah, GA 31401
Directions: From I-95 take exit 17 to I-16. Go east on I-16 to the city of Savannah, where I-16 becomes Montgomery Street. Continue on Montgomery Street until you make a right turn onto W. Oglethorpe Avenue, then go six blocks and make a left turn onto Abercorn Street. Continue until you reach Oglethorpe Square.
Hours: 10:00 a.m. to 5:00 p.m. Tuesday to Saturday; 2:00 p.m. to 5:00 p.m. Sunday and Monday
Closed: January and major holidays
Admission fee: yes
Wheelchair access: garden, yes; house, partial
Facilities: gift shop
Area: 1/8 acre
Phone: (912) 233-9743

This house, considered by many as the finest example of English Regency architecture in America, was designed by English architect William Jay. Commissioned by the prominent banker and cotton merchant Richard Richardson and his wife, the house was completed in 1819. Unfortunately the Richardsons did not enjoy their house for long; they lost it in the economic depression of 1820. Over the next decade the house was used as an elegant boarding house. From the balcony of this house the Revolutionary War hero Marquis de Lafayette spoke to the people of Savannah during his triumphant return in 1825. In 1830, George W. Owens, mayor of Savannah, lawyer, and congressman, purchased the property, and the house remained in the family until 1951, when Owens's granddaughter, Margaret Thomas, bequeathed it to the Telfair Academy of Arts and Sciences. It is a National Historic Landmark.

The recreation of the1820s garden, designed by Clermont Lee, was added in the 1950s. It is a small English Regency garden with its formal symmetry, four beautifully sculptured and trimmed **Japanese ligustrums** (*Ligustrum japonicum*), and a central fountain. The garden is surrounded by walls of tabby (a concrete-like mixture of oyster shells, lime, and sand) and brick, with walkways made of ballast stones of ships. Clipped borders of native **Georgia holly** and plantings of **azaleas, wisteria, junipers, Lady Banksia rose,** and **Cherokee roses** round out the setting.

Cherokee rose (*Rosa laevigata*), a native of China and Taiwan, is believed to have been introduced into the South by Spanish missionaries. It has naturalized in the South to such an extent that it was adopted as the state flower of Georgia. The rose is a vigorous climber with stems containing respectable thorns. It blossoms in late March to April with single, large, pure white, five-petaled flowers that are intensely fragrant.

Worth Seeing: Treat yourself to a tour of the **Richardson-Owens-Thomas House.** This elegant townhouse represents a wonderful combination of English design and usage of native materials. The house's design follows a Regency-influenced symmetry, where every feature of the house has its corresponding opposite. On the outside, two curving stairways lead to the front door; on the inside, dual staircases lead from the main hall to the upper floor. Where one door was designed for its function, another one was put in to create a symmetrical effect. The plaster trompe l'oeil in the corners of the drawing room creates an optical illusion of a circular ceiling in a square room. Constructed largely of tabby, it also features the first large-scale use of cast iron in the region. The cast-iron railings and columns of the south balcony are the earliest and finest examples of local ornamental ironwork. An ingenious and elaborate plumbing system provided the house with running water, baths, and water closets, making it one of the most sophisticated in early nineteenth-century America. An outstanding collection of decorative arts and furnishings adorns the interior of the house.

The carriage house features the best-preserved urban slave quarters remaining in the United States.

Green-Meldrim House

Three small gardens surround this national historic landmark.

Address: 14 West Macon Street, Savannah, GA 31401
Directions: From I-95 take exit 17 to I-16. Go east on I-16 to the
    city of Savannah, where I-16 becomes Montgomery Street. Make
    an almost immediate right turn onto W. Charlton Street and go
    for five blocks until reaching Madison Square, where the house is
    located.
Hours: 10:00 a.m. to 4:00 p.m. Tuesday, Thursday and Friday;
    10:00 a.m. to 1:00 p.m. Saturday
Closed: Monday, Wednesday, Sunday, and all major holidays
Admission fee: donation
Wheelchair access: no
Facilities: none
Area: 1/4 acre
Phone: (912) 233-3845

The house, designed by architect John S. Norris and built in 1853 for the English cotton merchant Charles Green, represents one of the finest examples of Gothic Revival architecture in the South. The elaborate ironwork, especially of its balconies, is quite unique and very impressive. During the Civil War, when Union troops occupied Savannah, Mr. Green offered the house to General William Tecumseh Sherman for use as his headquarters. He accepted, and it was from this house in December 1864 that General Sherman sent his famous telegram to President Lincoln offering him the city of Savannah as a Christmas gift.

An interesting footnote—Mr. Green, as a British subject, required
General Sherman to pay rent while using his house, which Sherman
apparently did. Later on the house was purchased by the Meldrim
family who lived in it until 1943. The house is now the parish house
of St. John's Episcopal Church. It is a National Historic Landmark.

There are three gardens here, two surrounding the house and one
as a part of The Cloister.

The **Parish House Garden**, a small garden of authentic 1850s
parterre design, is enclosed by the original iron fence. Follow pearock
paths bordered with bricks, **boxwood hedges,** and **lilies**.
Surrounding **live oaks** and **Southern magnolias** provide welcome
shade.

The **Rectory Garden** is walled in under the **Chinese tallow
tree** (*Sapium sebiferum*) with a small reflecting pool and brick-
bordered flagstone walkways.

The **Cloister Garden,** of simple layout, provides a foreground
for the church and Cloister arches. In the center is a reflecting pool
with fountain, surrounded by lawn bordered by **azaleas** and clipped
boxwood hedges.

Worth Seeing: Take a tour of **Green-Meldrim House**. See elaborate plaster moldings, fireplace mantles of Carrara marble, Austrian
mirrors, and wood finishes of black walnut.

William Scarbrough House

A recently restored garden surrounds this historical house. Many plantings are relatively recent, but the giant sycamore trees are believed to be the oldest in Savannah.

Address: 41 Martin Luther King Jr. Boulevard, Savannah, GA 31401

Directions: From I-95 take exit 17 to I-16. Go east on I-16 to the city of Savannah, where it becomes Montgomery Street. Continue on Montgomery Street to Franklin Square where you make a left turn onto W. Bryan Street. Go for one block and make a left turn onto Martin Luther King Boulevard. The house will be on your right.

Hours: 10:00 a.m. to 5:00 p.m. Tuesday to Sunday

Closed: Mondays and major holidays

Admission fee: yes

Wheelchair access: gardens, yes; house, no

Facilities: gift shop

Area: 1/4 acre

Phone: (912) 232-1511

By designing this house, English architect William Jay created one of the earliest examples of Greek Revival architecture in the South. The house was built in 1819 for William Scarbrough, principal owner of the SS *Savannah*, the first steamship to cross the Atlantic Ocean. William and Julia Scarbrough received President James Monroe in this house while he was in Savannah on his Southern tour. Then many turbulent years followed. Starting in the 1870s, the house was used for many years as a public school. It even became abandoned for about twenty years. Finally it was restored by the Historic Savannah Foundation in the 1970s. Then another period of neglect followed until the last restoration in 1996–97. Now the house serves as the headquarters for the Ships of the Sea Maritime Museum. It is listed on the National Register of Historic Places.

The garden was initially restored by the Trustees' Garden Club, and then further enlarged in 1997. There are new plantings of

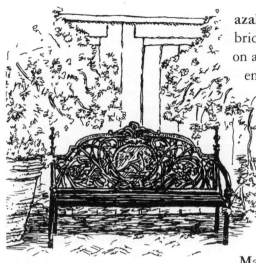

azaleas and **laurels** alongside brick pathways. You can sit on a wrought-iron bench and enjoy **roses** climbing brick walls. Many plantings are recent but giant **sycamore trees,** believed to be oldest in city of Savannah, provide the shade.

Worth Seeing: Visit the **Ships of the Sea Maritime Museum,** located in the Scarbrough House, which showcases exhibits relating to the grand era of cross-Atlantic trade and travel during the 1700s and 1800s. The museum features large-scale models of the great ships, maritime antiques, paintings, and a variety of other seafaring artifacts. Video presentations are also available.

The Trustees' Garden

Address: 20 East Broad Street, Savannah, GA 31401

Just the historical marker can be seen; there is no garden here to explore. But this site, maybe more than anything else, exemplifies the tradition of gardening in Georgia.

Within one month of his arrival in 1733, General James Oglethorpe established a ten-acre garden and named it in honor of the English trustees of the last colony. This first public experimental garden in America was closely modeled after the Chelsea Physic Garden in London. Botanists were sent by the trustees of the colony from England all over the world to obtain plants and cuttings for the garden. Soon fruit trees, olives, flax, hemp, indigo, and medicinal spices were beginning to grow. Vine cuttings and mulberry trees were carefully tended with high hopes of establishing the wine industry and silk culture. The silk and wine industries failed to materialize due to weather conditions and unsuitable soil. But upland cotton and peach trees propagated and disseminated from this garden became Georgia's major commercial crops. In 1755 the garden was closed, and the site was developed into a residential section.

When exploring Savannah, try visualizing this garden, defined to the north by Savannah River, to the east by old Fort Wayne, to the south by what is now Broughton Street, and to the west by what is now East Broad Street.

Chatham County Garden Center and Botanical Gardens

There are several distinct gardens to enjoy here, all beautifully tended by volunteers from area garden clubs.

Address: 1388 Eisenhower Drive, Savannah, GA 31406

Directions: From I-95 take exit 16 and go east on SR 204 for about eleven miles. Make a right turn onto Eisenhower Drive and go for about 1.2 miles. The garden entrance will be on your left.

Hours: Gardens open daily from sunrise to sunset. The center is open Monday to Friday 10:00 a.m. to 2:00 p.m.

Admission fee: donation

Wheelchair access: yes

Facilities: none

Available: tours of the house and gardens for a nominal fee

Area: 10.5 acres

Phone: (912) 355-3883

The botanical gardens here are fairly young, and when you look around and see the lovely gardens with all the beautiful blossoms, you would never believe this once was a prison. Savannah Area Council of Garden Clubs, Inc., a nonprofit organization, was able to obtain a long-term lease from Chatham County on the property once used as a prison farm. In 1991 the development of gardens was started with the following objectives:

- to promote the wise use of natural resources;
- to plant, preserve and study native trees, shrubs, and flowers;

- to further educate the public sector in fields of conservation, civic beautification, horticulture, litter control, garden therapy and landscape design;
- to offer students archeological study areas, nature trails, and outdoor classrooms;
- to schedule lectures and courses in horticulture, floral design, environmental awareness, landscape design, and other garden related subjects;
- to schedule guided tours of botanical gardens and the 1840s farmhouse, which serves as garden center headquarters.

In 1992, the historic 1840s Helmken Street farmhouse, slated for demolition to make a way for a new road, was moved to the gardens. The structure was restored and now serves as the garden center head-quarters and administrative office, and also houses the garden research library. The gardens opened to the public unofficially in 1993 and officially in May 1997.

There are several gardens here to enjoy, all beautifully main-tained and tended by volunteers from area garden clubs. Featured are **Camellia Garden, Azalea Garden,** and **Scent Garden**. During our April visit the **Rose Garden** was at its blooming peak and looking extremely impressive. See the nearby **Fall Garden, Summer Garden,** as well as **Winter and Spring Gardens**. Do not miss the **Herb Parterre, Kitchen Garden,** or **Perennial Garden**. And as you start following nature trails, you will discover **Shade Garden, Wildflower Meadow, Fern Garden,** and **Bog Garden**. You will walk through **Pine & Sweetgum Forest,** and do not miss the **Native Plants** area. There is plenty to see in this garden, so take your time and enjoy.

Coastal Gardens

Forty-six-acre garden with the largest collection of bamboo in North America. And it's not just bamboo. Their collections of daylilies and crape myrtles are outstanding as well.

Address: 2 Canebrake Road, Savannah, GA 31419
Directions: From I-95 take exit 16 and go east on SR 204 for about 1.5 miles. Make a right turn onto US 17 and go south for about one mile. The garden entrance will be on your right.
Hours: Daily from sunrise to sunset. Gardens office is open 8:00 a.m. to 4:00 p.m. Monday to Friday.
Admission fee: no
Wheelchair access: partial
Facilities: conference center, open-air pavilion, gift shop
Available: membership, educational programs, guided tours by appointment
Area: 46 acres
Phone: (912) 921-5460

In 1890, Mrs. H. B. Miller planted three small bamboo plants given to her by a Cuban rice planter living near Georgia's Ogeechee River. Mrs. Miller's plants grew and grew on what became locally known as "Bamboo Farm." In 1915, this bamboo grove attracted the attention of Dr. David Fairchild, head of the United States Department of Agriculture's Seed and Plant Introduction Section, an agency he also created. Dr. Fairchild was one of the most distinguished plant collectors, botanists, and horticulturists of his time. He was responsible for the introduction of more than two thousand different species of plants into the United States. Although most of his introductions were tropical fruits, he also brought in a multitude of palms, vines, flowering trees, and grains. Many plants commonly grown today and many food staples present on our kitchen tables were his new introductions: polyembryonic mangos from Indonesia; cotton and dates from Egypt; rice, soybeans, and cherry trees from Japan; wheat from Russia; and cauliflower from Italy. The beauty and economic value of bamboo also fascinated him.

Dr. Fairchild interested world-traveler Barbour Lathrop, his longtime friend and travel companion, in this farm. Eventually, Barbour Lathrop bought the entire farm and donated it to the Department of Agriculture. The farm was officially accepted by an act of Congress in 1919. For the next sixty years, the Barbour Lathrop Plant Introduction Garden thrived and prospered. Countless plants were received and planted here, and if found suitable, distributed to areas of United States that had similar climates. The farm was closed in 1978 as a part of cost containment efforts. The property was acquired by the University of Georgia and became a center for research and education. The University of Georgia Cooperative Extension Service took over the operation of the center in 1983, renaming it the Coastal Area Extension Center. In 1994 the center was renamed Coastal Gardens to better reflect its mission. Coastal Gardens today is an important resource for coastal Georgia, offering educational programs and resources as well as conference facilities to the public. And today, more than one hundred years later, what started as three small plants have become more than two acres of **Japanese giant timber bamboo**.

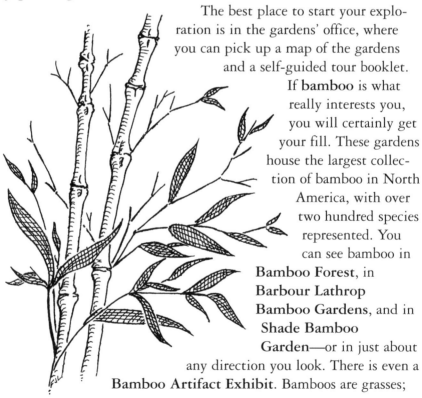

The best place to start your exploration is in the gardens' office, where you can pick up a map of the gardens and a self-guided tour booklet. If **bamboo** is what really interests you, you will certainly get your fill. These gardens house the largest collection of bamboo in North America, with over two hundred species represented. You can see bamboo in **Bamboo Forest**, in **Barbour Lathrop Bamboo Gardens**, and in **Shade Bamboo Garden**—or in just about any direction you look. There is even a **Bamboo Artifact Exhibit**. Bamboos are grasses;

some have woody stems and may range in height from a few inches to more than one hundred feet. Many kinds of bamboo are cultivated for their ornamental value, yet very few plants offer more practical uses than bamboo. The young shoots and seeds of some bamboos are edible. The wood is used for a multitude of building materials: furniture, mats, and paper are just a few of the additional uses. And some of the bamboos grow amazingly fast, easily a foot per day. For example, **giant timber bamboo** (*Phyllostachys bambusoides*) can reach a height of more than seventy feet and it can reach it in just forty to sixty days.

But there is more than just bamboo. Keep in mind that for more than sixty years all sorts of plants, gathered by botanists and plant experts all over the world, were sent and planted here. Several of them are the only specimens of their kind in North America.

Crape Myrtle Collection is probably the largest collection of **crape myrtles** (*Lagerstroemia indica*) in coastal Georgia. The range of their colors is just amazing. When you see **Daylily Garden** you will agree that the collection of **daylilies** (*Hemerocallis*) is quite remarkable. It is said to contain more than six hundred varieties. During May, you can see their color spectrum—from white, yellow, and pink to orange, lavender, and red. Several varieties have blossoms combining many of the colors.

Magnolia Collection contains sixteen varieties of **Southern magnolias**. **Herb Gardens** contains fifty varieties of cultivated herbs. There are extensive vegetable gardens, blackberries, strawberry fields, and a grape arbor. And what about the **Persimmon Collection, Pear Orchard,** demonstration plots of **turf** and **ornamental grasses**, or **summer and fall/winter annuals** for a splash of color. The list could go on and on. When you come to visit here, who knows what you may discover.

Guido Gardens

Gardens surrounding the Sower Studio are especially beautiful during the spring. Your garden visit will be accompanied by inspirational music.

Address: P. O. Box 508, Metter, GA 30439
Directions: From I-16 take exit 23 and go north on SR 23/121 for about three miles. The entrance will be on your right, at 600 North Lewis Street.
Hours: Gardens never close
Admission fee: no
Wheelchair access: yes
Facilities: none
Area: 3.5 acres
Phone: (912) 685-2222

The quiet little farming town of Metter is home to Guido Gardens, and Guido Gardens is home to the Sower Studio, where Dr. Michael A. Guido produces radio broadcasts and telecasts for the nondenominational Guido Evangelistic Association, Inc. The gardens were developed in the 1970s and are still continuing to evolve and improve. Anytime is the best time to visit since the gardens never close. As with any Southern garden, the spring blossoms are the most spectacular. You can enjoy a multitude of **native Georgia plants,** including **azaleas, pines, dogwoods,** and **magnolias.** Follow the brick paths, walk over the wooden bridges, and look at the reflecting pools. Enjoy **Sower Topiary Garden, Tea House,** and **Garden Shelter.** All of this is accompanied by inspirational music.

Georgia Southern Botanical Garden

This new botanical garden emphasizes plants native to the Georgia coastal plain. The exquisite camellia collection will fascinate you.

Address: P. O. Box 8039, Statesboro, GA 30460

Directions: From I-16 take exit 26 and go north on SR 67 for about twelve miles. SR 67 becomes Fair Road. Make a left turn onto Georgia Avenue, then a right turn onto Bland Avenue. The entrance to the garden parking lot will be on your right.

Hours: The garden gates and Bland Cottage visitor's center are open weekdays 9:00 a.m. to 5:30 p.m. and Sundays 2:00 p.m. to 5:00 p.m. all year except university holidays. The garden grounds are open daily from sunrise to sunset.

Admission fee: no

Wheelchair access: yes

Facilities: visitor's center, gift shop

Available: group tours, memberships, lecturers, classes and workshops

Area: 11 acres

Phone: (912) 871-1114

Located just two blocks south of the main campus of the university is this young botanical garden. The garden was actually born in the mid-1980s, when the longtime home and farm of Dan and Catharine Bland were bequeathed to Georgia Southern University to be developed as a botanical garden and wildlife preserve. Don Bland, an amateur naturalist, was very much interested in plants and animals native to this region. And today, Georgia Southern Botanical Garden emphasizes plants native to the Georgia coastal plain. The primary goal of the garden "is to increase knowledge and appreciation of southeast Georgia's plants and animals through its collections, exhibits and educational activities."

You may start your visit at the Bland Cottage; take a look at the displays there, pick up a visitor's guide containing a garden map, and you are on your way. Look down the allée of **Southern magnolia** (*Magnolia grandiflora*) and **American holly** (*Ilex opaca*) extending northeast from the cottage. The allée was planted in the 1940s. **Woodland Trails** extend to the north and south of the allée. Follow the trails under the canopy of **longleaf pine** (*Pinus palustris*), **eastern red cedar** (*Juniperus virginiana*), and **green ash** (*Fraxinus pennsylvanica*) to name just a few. Wooded areas here are planted with understory native species characteristic of mixed hardwood and pine forests. Labels and interpretive signs will help you with identification. We especially enjoyed the displays of **native azaleas**, namely *Rhododendron canescens* and *Rhododendron atlanticum*. The **Arboretum** features plantings of trees and shrubs native to the Georgia coastal plain. **Tully Pennington Camellia Collection** showcases a variety of **camellias** planted by Mr. Bland as well as many varieties planted recently. In **Butterfly Border**, plants were selected to attract not just butterflies, but bees and birds as well. Do not forget to see **Children's Vegetable Garden** or the **Heritage Zone** featuring **Bland Cottage** and the farm buildings. There is plenty to see here, and keep in mind that the garden is continuously expanding and improving.

Plains Region

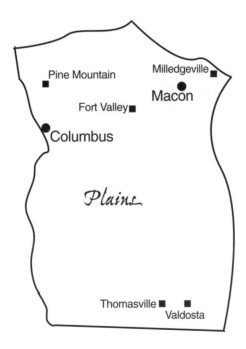

Pine Mountain ■

Milledgeville ■

● Macon

Fort Valley ■

● Columbus

Plains

Thomasville ■   ■
Valdosta

The Crescent

The formal garden offers boxwood hedges and brick pathways, blossoms of dogwoods, and azaleas and redbuds during the spring, all surrounded by old live oaks draped in Spanish moss.

Address: 904 North Patterson Street, P.O. Box 2423, Valdosta, GA 31604

Directions: From I-75 take exit 4 and go east on US 84 for about 2.4 miles. Make a left turn onto Toombs Street and proceed for about 0.7 miles, then make a right turn on Gordon Street. The Crescent entrance will be in the middle of the block on your left.

Hours: Grounds open year-round. The house is open Monday to Friday 2:00 p.m. to 5:00 p.m. and by appointment.

Closed: Saturday, Sunday, and most major holidays

Admission fee: donation accepted for house tour

Wheelchair access: garden, yes; house, first floor only

Facilities: none

Area: 3/4 acre

Phone: (912) 244-6747

South Georgia's Valdosta is a city with a rich heritage; its three historic districts feature many fine buildings of the Victorian era. There is a collection of beautifully restored houses on Patterson Street, and The Crescent is one of them. This twenty-three-room mansion was completed in 1898 for William S. West.

Built in neoclassical style, it features a crescent-shaped, marble-and-tile front porch. It is believed that the thirteen Doric columns that support the portico represent the thirteen original colonies. William S. West was a successful businessman, farmer, teacher, and lawyer who amassed a fortune. He also served for many years in the Georgia legislature and was president of the Georgia Senate. Not all went well in later years. In the 1930s the West family suffered a reversal of fortune coupled with the depression that was gripping the nation. The mansion was divided into apartments, and by 1950 the situation was so bad that the building was slated to be razed to make space for a gas station. The thought of losing one of the city's most distinctive landmarks caused three dedicated women to spearhead a fundraising drive to raise the money to purchase and save the mansion. The idea was to establish The Crescent as headquarters for the city's several garden clubs. The money needed was raised in just two months. Restored and refurbished, The Crescent was listed in the National Register of Historic Places in 1980. Today it is owned by the Valdosta Garden Center, Inc., which is made up of the following seven garden clubs: Amaryllis Garden Club, Azalea Garden Club, Camellia Garden Club, Dogwood Garden Club, Holly Garden Club, Magnolia Garden Club, and the Town and Country Garden Club.

Stately old **live oaks** draped in **Spanish moss** surround the property. Blossoms of **azaleas, dogwoods,** and **redbuds** provide the color display during the spring. The formal garden with its **boxwood hedges** and brick pathways incorporates a variety of plants into its design. Enjoy **roses, amaryllis,** and **lilies**. The central fountain and pool add a pleasing water element, and the pergola features vines that thrive in the climate of southern Georgia. The entire garden is beautifully tended, and all plants throughout the garden are clearly marked.

Worth Seeing: Take the house tour of **The Crescent**. The house is furnished in period and has a large ballroom with an orchestra alcove, numerous fireplaces, and ornate woodwork.

The octagonal schoolhouse was built in 1913 and formerly housed a progressive kindergarten. It is one of the few remaining buildings of its kind in the state.

Thomasville Rose Garden

Although covering only a half acre, the garden's six hundred rose bushes explode into a multitude of blossoms just in time for the annual Rose Show and Festival in mid-April.

Address: Destination Thomasville Tourism Authority, P. O. Box 1540, Thomasville, GA 31799
Directions: From I-75 take exit 4 and go west for about forty miles on US 84 to Thomasville. Make a right turn onto Covington Street; the garden will be on your left.
Hours: Open daily from sunrise to sunset
Admission fee: no
Wheelchair access: yes
Facilities: none
Area: 1/2 acre
Phone: (912) 225-3919 or (800) 704-2350

Right in Thomasville, within sight of Cherokee Lake, surrounded by oaks, magnolias, and pines, lies the Thomasville Rose Garden. Yes, Thomasville really is the "City of Roses," as it has been known since the 1920s. Peter J. Hjort, a Danish immigrant, started the rose nursery in 1898, and his first catalog of roses was printed in 1921. Soon, his nurseries were shipping roses and plants all over the United States. In 1953 the nursery became the testing site for an All-American Rose Selection Garden, a trial garden where roses would be evaluated for disease resistance, hardiness, and overall appeal to gardeners. After ninety-six years in business, the nursery closed its doors in 1994. The Thomasville municipal government felt that the "City of Roses" needed a public rose garden and decided to create one.

And what a garden they created. Over six hundred individual rose bushes can be found here. From **old-fashioned roses**, to **floribunda, grandiflora, hybrid tea, miniature, climber,** and **shrub roses**—they all thrive here. Enjoy the central Victorian rose garden gazebo and arbor garden shelters with seating nooks. There is a **butterfly garden** as well. Roses start blooming by mid-April, just in time for the annual **Rose Show and Festival**. Do not miss it.

Pebble Hill Plantation

Approach the main plantation house along a winding drive lined with magnificent live oaks and southern magnolias. Enjoy the formal gardens as well as spectacular blossoms of flowering trees during the spring.

Address: P. O. Box 830, Thomasville, GA 31799

Directions: From I-75 take exit 4 and go west on US 84 for almost forty-two miles to Thomasville. Then go south on Rt. 319, and after about six miles the entrance to the plantation will be on your right.

Hours: 10:00 a.m. to 5:00 p.m. Tuesday through Saturday; 1:00 p.m. to 5:00 p.m. Sunday

Closed: Mondays, the day after Labor Day to October 1, Thanksgiving, Christmas Eve, Christmas Day, and New Year's Day

Admission fee: yes

Wheelchair access: yes

Facilities: gift shop

Available: guided tours

Area: 3,000 acres; museum and grounds, 34 acres

Phone: (912) 226-2344

Pebble Hill Plantation is located near Thomasville, in southwest Georgia's Thomas County, not far from the Florida border. It is the only plantation, out of more than seventy in the area, that is regularly open to the public for tours. Thomas County was formed in 1825 by legislation introduced by Thomas Jefferson Johnson, who also founded the city of Thomasville. It is believed both city and county are named for General Jet Thomas, who was a member of the state militia during the War of 1812. Thomas Jefferson Johnson built the first house on Pebble Hill in the mid-1820s. Johnson's daughter, Julia Ann, eventually inherited the plantation and married a local planter, John H. Mitchell. In 1850, the Mitchells replaced the original house with a new one, designed by English architect John Wind. Pebble Hill Plantation started as a working plantation, growing a variety of crops, mainly cotton and tobacco. John H. Mitchell also invented a unique irrigation system that allowed Pebble Hill Plantation to become one of the largest rice-producing plantations in the entire county. The cotton-planting operations were also expanded. After the Civil War, hard economic times hit all the plantations in this region, and Pebble Hill was no exception. After the death of her husband, Julia Ann continued to run the plantation until her own passing.

Anxious to restart the area economy, Thomasville began an extraordinary campaign in the Northern cities to advertise its healthy, pine-scented climate and pleasant, mild winters. The response was phenomenal; during the 1880s, Thomasville developed a reputation as a resort destination for wealthy Northerners. Then the railroad arrived, a spur conveniently terminating at the Thomasville depot, and the area really started to boom. Wealthy industrialists started to buy undervalued cotton plantations and convert them into hunting estates. The plantations were full of wild game; quail hunting especially was spectacular. Still others were buying land to build their own winter homes. Some of the most luxuriously appointed hotels of the entire country opened up in Thomasville, the "Original Winter Resort of the South." The boom disappeared in the early 1900s when the railroad spur, which until then had gone no farther than Thomasville, was extended south into Florida. So the railroad that brought the golden goose also took it away, ending the "Grand Hotel Era." Many Northern tourists then continued right through Thomasville to the even warmer climates of Palm Beach and Miami.

But the hunting plantations remained in the hands of their owners, too affluent to be affected by the reversal of fortunes in Thomasville. Howard Melville Hanna, a Cleveland, Ohio, industrialist, started to purchase land in Thomas

County in the late 1800s and eventually accumulated thousands of acres and several plantations. He purchased Pebble Hill Plantation in 1896. Later on Hanna gave the

plantation to his daughter, Kate, who converted a working plantation into a family winter home and hunting estate. She also commissioned Abram Garfield, son of President James Garfield, to design
and build gatehouses and several other additions to the property. The
glory days of Pebble Hill Plantation were restored again. In 1934 the
main house was destroyed by fire; only the east wing was left
standing. Abram Garfield was again commissioned to design a new
main house that would incorporate the surviving east wing. The
twenty-eight-room house, in Georgian and Greek Revival style, was
completed in 1936. After Kate's death, her daughter, Elizabeth
"Pansy" Ireland, inherited the plantation. During the Hanna years
many notables were guests at the Pebble Hill Plantation: presidents,
royalty, and artists. Before Miss Pansy died, she established a private
Pebble Hill Foundation to operate the plantation after her death. So
according to her wishes, the plantation was opened to the public,
and the main plantation house was turned into a museum.

After entering, you approach the main plantation house by a
winding drive, lined first with magnificent **live oaks** and then with
Southern magnolias. Gardens, located in front of the main house,
with their formal symmetry, walkways of brick set in geometrical
patterns and hedged by **boxwood,** will lead you through plantings
of **azaleas** and **camellias.** Spectacular **live oaks, Southern magnolias,** and **pines** surround the gardens. During our spring visit,
dogwoods with their snowy white blossoms were magnificent, and
the approaching storm that day made the fragrance of **wisteria**
permeating the air even more intense.

Worth seeing: Take a guided tour of the **house,** where living areas
look virtually the same as when Miss Pansy lived there. There are
paintings by renowned American and British artists, and a large
collection of dog and horse art. Most of the artwork here features
animals and scenes from nature. The collection also includes thirty-
three original John J. Audubon prints. There are fine antiques here, as
well as collections of silver, crystal, and porcelain.

A self-guided tour of the grounds begins at the **Visitors' Center,**
where one can view an orientation film or exhibits on the plantation
history. The **Map and Touring Guide** will lead you around the property while giving you directions and information about the stables,
the carriage house, kennels, and many other plantation structures.

Massee Lane Gardens

This ten-acre garden boasts probably the finest camellia collection in the world. But that's not all, come and you will see.

Address: One Massee Lane, Fort Valley, GA 31030
Directions: From I-75 take exit 46 and go on SR 49 to Ft. Valley. Continue about five miles past Ft. Valley, and Massee Lane will be on your left side.
Hours: December to March: 9:00 a.m. to 5:00 p.m. Monday to Saturday, 1:00 p.m. to 5:00 p.m. Sunday. April to November: 9:00 a.m. to 4:00 p.m. Monday to Friday.
Closed: major holidays
Admission fee: yes
Wheelchair access: yes
Facilities: gift shop
Available: Workshops, classes on horticulture, a Discover Nature Camp for children offered each summer, guided tours by prior appointment. The library, containing the world's largest collection of books on camellias, is available for research by appointment.
Area: 10 acres
Phone: (912) 967-2358 or (912) 967-2722

Surrounded by **pecan groves** and **peach orchards,** not far from Fort Valley, Massee Lane Gardens is the home of the American Camellia Society. The site was once a large plantation originally acquired by Needham Massee in the 1820s. In the early 1900s Mr. D. C. Strother purchased a small part of former plantation acreage for farmland. He became fascinated with **camellias,** began planting them on his property in the 1930s, and started to create his own private camellia garden. He was also instrumental in founding the American Camellia Society in 1945. This not-for-profit educational, scientific, and charitable corporation is dedicated to the study and promotion of the genus *Camellia*. Its present membership consists of camellia enthusiasts and lovers from forty-four U.S. states and twenty-two foreign countries. Mr. Strother donated his gardens and farm to the American Camellia Society, and Massee Lane Gardens became the society's headquarters in 1968.

Nestled under the towering tall **pines** that provide shade are over two thousand **camellias**; this garden without question features one of the finest camellia collections in the world. Why not begin your tour with the fifteen-minute slide presentation, which will give you an overview of camellias and the American Camellia Society. After that, you are ready to explore. Brick pathways with an occasional old millstone incorporated in the path design will lead you through the gardens. Plantings of camellias can be enjoyed throughout the gardens, but do not forget to see the large landscaped greenhouse containing over two hundred camellia varieties.

Camellias, of course, are the main attraction, and they bloom from November to March. You will be amazed by the spectrum of colors. But there is more to Massee Lane Gardens than just camellias.

Delightful specialty gardens are waiting to be discovered. **Scheibert Rose Garden** will add still more to the color and fragrance experience, while **Abendroth Japanese Garden** offers a place for quiet reflection. Then there are **Entry Garden, Formal Garden,** and **Awards Garden** to see. If you cannot visit during the camellia blooming season, do not despair—visit anyway! There is plenty of seasonal color provided throughout the gardens: from **flowering trees, dogwoods, azaleas,** collections of **daffodils, narcissus, and daylilies,** to **chrysanthemums, annuals,** and **perennials.** You will find your visit here truly enjoyable.

Worth Seeing:

Stevens Taylor Gallery displays the world's largest and most complete collection of Edward Marshall Boehm's porcelains. Donated by Mildred Taylor Stevens of Macon, Georgia, this collection of more than one hundred pieces of mainly birds and flowers showcases some of his earlier work.

Annabelle Lundy Fetterman Educational Museum is housed in a beautiful Georgian-style building that also serves as the visitor center for the gardens. An additional collection of porcelains, primarily rare large pieces and sculptures, is displayed here. In addition to Boehm's porcelains, there are also works of other renowned artists such as Sister Maria Innocentia Hummel, Boleslaw Cybis, and Susan Dorothy Dougherty.

Lockerly Arboretum

This forty-seven-acre arboretum features more than six thousand species of plants—from azaleas, rhododendrons, and flowering trees to conifers and camellias. And that is just the beginning of what you can see here.

Address: 1534 Irwington Road, Milledgeville, GA 31061

Directions: From I-16 take exit 14 and go north on US 441 until Milledgeville. Stay on US 441 and follow signs; the entrance to the arboretum will be on your right. From I-20 take exit 51 and go south on US 441 for about thirty miles to Milledgeville. Stay on US 441 throughout the entire city. US 441 eventually will become Irwington Road. Watch for the signs. The entrance to the arboretum will be on your left.

Hours: October to May: Monday to Friday 8: 30 a.m. to 4:30 p.m.; Saturdays 1:00 p.m. to 5:00 p.m. June to September: 10:00 a.m. to 2:00 p.m.

Closed: Sundays and some holidays

Admission fee: no

Wheelchair access: partial

Facilities: none

Available: guided group tours by prior appointment

Area: 47 acres

Phone: (912) 452-2112

Located in the middle of Georgia in quiet Milledgeville, Lockerly Arboretum presents an unexpectedly pleasant find. Its origins go back to the 1960s. Mr. Edward J. Grassmann, a businessman, amateur naturalist, and ornithologist, was a frequent visitor to this area. He established Georgia Kaolin Co. and later on donated funds to purchase the land for what was to became Lockerly Arboretum. The arboretum is a private, nonprofit educational and research entity operated by the Lockerly Arboretum Foundation, Inc., which was chartered in 1965.

More than six thousand species of plants can be seen here—not only plants native to the area, but plants from all over the world. To experiment with plants native to other regions and to study their growth in the climate and soil of mid-Georgia are some of the arboretum's objectives. The arboretum truly is a horticultural laboratory rather than a showplace garden. There are many sections of the arboretum to be explored, and the best place to start is the office. Pick up your map and trail guide there, and you are ready to start your tour. There are several walking **nature trails** as well as roadways to lead you into every corner of the arboretum.

We started our exploration by admiring the collection of **rhododendrons** displaying their showy flowers. More than three hundred of their cultivars thrive here. Native **azaleas** are displayed along the shaded walking trail under the canopy of tall trees. The **Piedmont azalea** (*Rhododendron canescens*) is the most abundant of all native azalea species, showcasing its intensely fragrant blossoms usually in late March to early April. Farther along the trail, the white, rose, or pink blossoms of **mountain laurel** (*Kalmia latifolia*) were quite spectacular.

Hybrid Azalea Collection is located along the entrance drive, and more than three hundred azaleas can be enjoyed in this area. **Conifer Collection** covers five acres and contains more than three hundred conifers (cone-bearing plants). There is a section of **flowering trees;** we admired nice specimens of **Southern magnolia** (*Magnolia grandiflora*) and **bigleaf magnolia** (*Magnolia macrophylla*).

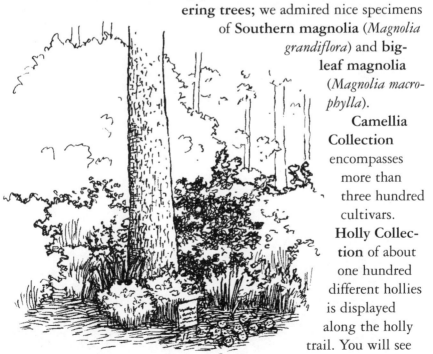

Camellia Collection encompasses more than three hundred cultivars. **Holly Collection** of about one hundred different hollies is displayed along the holly trail. You will see evergreen and **deciduous hollies** in shrub or tree forms. The spring-fed pond is the area to see **shore, bog,** and **aquatic plants:** a carpet of **water lilies,** a profusion of **irises,** and a variety of colors everywhere. Blossoms of **sacred lotus** (*Nelumbium nucifera*) were just breathtaking. Recently a collection of **carnivorous plants** was added to this area. Do not forget to see **Iris Collection** containing thousands of irises including over six hundred different hybrids. You will be astounded by the spectrum of their colors and shapes. Their peak blooming period is during the months of April and May. **Butterfly Garden** is planted with a selection of plants attractive to butterflies, and you can expect to see all sorts of butterflies around the butterfly bed. **Herb Garden** is divided into three sections, covering medicinal, culinary, and fragrance herbs. **Developing Climax Forest** area provides a glimpse into the interactions of pines and hardwoods. And there are other collections to see—**Hawthorns, Ferns, Vineyards, Brambles, Viburnums, Hostas,** and **Pieris.** Tropical and desert greenhouses display over six hundred species of mostly exotic plants. There are even beehives to see, including a **glass observation hive** located inside the headquarters building. **Woods Museum** houses a very interesting collection of cut woods of native Georgia trees. There is so much here to see. Enjoy.

Callaway Gardens

Just imagine 2,500 acres of display gardens only about seventy miles south of Atlanta. Callaway Gardens is one of the most beautiful places you can imagine. From spectacular blossoms of azaleas and flowering trees in the spring to rhododendrons, beautiful summer colors, wildflowers, and other delights that fall and winter have to offer. Then there are the John A. Sibley Horticultural Center and Cecil B. Day Butterfly Center. Several miles of trails are waiting, so you can explore the gardens. This is without a doubt the finest facility in the South, combining beautiful public gardens with family-oriented recreational facilities.

Address: P. O. Box 2000, Pine Mountain, GA 31822

Directions: Driving south on I-85, take exit to I-185 and continue south to exit 14. Make a left turn onto US 27, and drive for about eleven miles to Callaway Gardens. Driving north on I-185, take exit 13 and go east for about eight miles on SR 18 to Pine Mountain. Make a right turn onto US 27 and go for about 1.7 miles. Callaway Gardens entrance will be on your right.

Hours: 7:00 a.m. to 7:00 p.m. daily from May to September. At other times hours may vary depending on scheduled events or season.

Admission fee: yes

Wheelchair access: partial

Facilities: Seven restaurants, inn, cottages, villas, convention center, several gift shops, golf, tennis, boating, fishing, biking and much more.

Available: educational workshops, lectures

Area: gardens, 2,500 acres; entire property, 14,000 acres

Phone: (800) 282-8181 or (706) 663-2281

Just seventy miles south of Atlanta lies Callaway Gardens—14,000 acres of gardens, lakes, streams, flowers, and woodlands adjacent to Pine Mountain Ridge. Cason J. Callaway was a wealthy cotton manufacturer, director of several major corporations, and a man of vision who originated the Georgia Better Farm Movement. Frequent visitors to this area since the early 1920s,

Callaway and his wife, Virginia, fell in love especially with the area around Blue Springs. On one of his summer hikes through the woods, Callaway discovered a wild growing shrub with beautiful red-orange blossoms. This was later identified as **plumleaf azalea.** This native azalea grows wild only within an approximately 100-mile radius of Pine Mountain. It is said that the discovery of plumleaf azalea convinced the Callaways to make their first land purchase here in 1930. Wanting to preserve the land they loved, they conceived the idea of creating a beautiful and restful place for the enjoyment of all people. Their dream became a reality when Callaway Gardens opened to the public on May 21, 1952.

And how better to explain Callaway Garden's philosophy than by quoting their own Mission Statement: "Callaway Gardens, a man-made landscape in a unique natural setting, was conceived and created by Cason J. Callaway and his wife, Virginia Hand Callaway, for the benefit of mankind. The purpose is to provide a wholesome family environment where all may find beauty, relaxation, inspiration and a better understanding of the living world. Callaway Gardens, a public, educational, horticultural and charitable organization, is owned and operated by the non-profit Ida Cason Callaway Foundation. Its wholly owned subsidiary, Callaway Gardens Resort, Inc., a regular business corporation, operates the recreational, lodging and retail facilities at Callaway Gardens. After-tax proceeds go to the Foundation to support its efforts."

There are many ways to go about exploring the gardens, as there are miles of **biking, walking,** and **hiking trails** and paved roads. They all offer access to the natural and horticultural display areas. Callaway Gardens places a great deal of emphasis on the preservation of native flora, and you certainly can enjoy plenty of it, as soon as you start to look around.

We would recommend the approach that worked quite well for us. Start with the five-mile **Scenic Drive**. That should give you an opportunity to get an overview of the gardens, to orient yourself and to identify specific areas of interest. The gardens cover a large area, and some plan of action is really necessary. As you drive around the gardens, please observe the speed limit. The speed limit is low; following it is not only safe, it is also the law. But above all, you will be richly rewarded for it.

During one of our visits, while driving slowly on a quiet morning, we came up on a family of foxes. We quietly stopped and observed the action. Mama fox with two of her young ones was quite nervously watching from the side of the road as the third and obviously smallest of the pups was sitting on his rump, in the middle of the road, chewing on a frog. We could not say whether the pup was trying to eat it or just play with it. The frog was all dried up and obviously had been dead for a long time. His mother was getting uneasy, and his two siblings seemed to have no idea what to do. The young pup was totally oblivious to us or to our car. That is, until we tried to reach for a camera on the back seat. Suddenly, they all disappeared. I have to report that the smallest pup did not forget to take his frog with him.

Let's first explore trails that were devoted to specific plant groups. But don't feel the trails are limited to those plants only. As you walk the trails and look around, depending on the season, you will see a profusion of colors and blossoms wherever you look: snowy white blossoms of native **dogwood trees** (*Cornus florida*) or purplish-pink blossoms of **redbud trees** (*Cercis canadensis*) in the spring; unforgettable blooms of **plumleaf azalea** (*Rhododendron prunifolium*) or masses of red **spider lilies** (*Lycoris radiata*) in the summer. You will see a surprising palette of color during the fall and winter as well.

But let's talk spring now, and spring in the South means **azaleas**. Callaway Gardens is almost synonymous with azaleas and probably the best place we know of to enjoy and admire them. Now, just a quick review of azaleas before getting on the trail. There are exotic oriental azaleas that are evergreen, deciduous native azaleas, and azalea hybrid groups. Exotic azaleas originated in the Orient and became very popular in Europe in the early 1800s, where they were primarily used as evergreen houseplants. Extensive azalea hybridization was conducted mainly in England and Belgium. The first exotic azaleas were planted in the South in the 1840s, and after more extensive introduction into the United States, they became immensely popular especially throughout the Southeast. Continuous selection and significant hybridization efforts over the years yielded various hybrid groups. The aim was to develop hybrids that would be more cold-hardy, blossom longer, or present different flower forms or colors. Deciduous azaleas, native to the southeastern United States, bloom from March through September. Their color range is spectacular, and the fragrances of some are extremely pleasing. Three azaleas bloom early in the spring, and all are pleasantly fragrant: **Piedmont azalea** (*Rhododendron canescens*) with white to pink blossoms, **Florida azalea** (*Rhododendron austrinum*) with yellow blossoms, and **coastal azalea** (*Rhododendron atlanticum*) blooming white. From mid to late spring you will see blossoming **Oconee azalea** (*Rhododendron flammeum*), which is yellow to orange, pink **pinkshell azalea** (*Rhododendron vaseyi*), and mostly white and quite fragrant **pinxterbloom azalea** (*Rhododendron periclymenoids*). During the late spring **Alabama azalea** (*Rhododendron alabamense*) displays its white, yellow-tinged, nicely scented flowers, while **Cumberland azalea** (*Rhododendron cumberlandense*) is orange-red. Summer blooming azaleas include mostly orange **plumleaf azalea** (*Rhododendron prunifolium*) and **flame azalea** (*Rhododendron calendulaceum*), which may be red, gold, or orange. And the following three summer azaleas are white and pleasantly fragrant: **sweet azalea** (*Rhododendron arborescens*), **swamp azalea** (*Rhododendron viscosum*) and **Hammocksweet azalea** (*Rhododendron serrulatum*).

Callaway Brothers Azalea Bowl Trail is the Callaway Gardens' newest addition. This 1.25-mile trail winds through the world's largest azalea garden, which is located between the **Ida Cason Callaway Memorial Chapel** and the **John A. Sibley Horticultural**

Center. This forty-acre garden features over 850 native azaleas representing 13 species and more than 3,400 hybrid azaleas representing about 100 varieties. There are also 2,000 trees and shrubs of approximately 120 varieties, not mentioning almost 15,000 of other plantings. Now that's impressive.

The **Azalea Trail,** winding its way through **Overlook Azalea Area,** is probably the best known. Located between and around **Whippoorwill** and **Mockingbird Lakes**, this area encompasses about twenty acres. Initially azaleas first planted in the gardens were deciduous species, native to the Southeast. Later on, other introduced species were added, mainly evergreen azaleas from Japan. The trail offers spectacular displays of azaleas planted in a natural woodland setting under the canopy of pines and hickories. Every spring visitors can wonder at the breathtaking display of thousands upon thousands of blossoms of every imaginable color and size. There are well over seven hundred species and varieties of azaleas thriving here, and this collection is one of the largest in the world. During our visit we were overwhelmed by the profusion of blossoms in the **Azalea Garden,** where plantings are arranged in a natural amphitheater, producing a truly striking effect. Of course, along the Azalea Trail azaleas steal the show, but there are plenty of other plants to enjoy. **Overlook Slope** features flowering shrubs and bulbs; companion plantings of other plants adapted to the same environment assure plenty of texture and color throughout the remainder of the year. So as spring passes and azalea blossoms slowly fade, other trails take the center stage.

The **Rhododendron Trail** really comes to life in late spring, usually from late April to mid-May. Colorful blossoms of many varieties of rhododendrons continue to amaze visitors. We especially enjoyed the huge clusters of pink, lavender or white flowers of **evergreen rhododendrons**. As you proceed along the trail, every turn will offer something new to see. Native **ferns, mahonias,** and **lily-of-the-valley** cover the ground. The trail eventually leads to a stone overlook, offering a vista of Hummingbird Lake as well as an opportunity to observe water birds.

The **Wildflower Trail** begins by the **Pioneer Log Cabin** and was one of the gardens' first trails. It reflects Virginia Callaway's interest in wildflowers and displays native plants of Georgia and the southeastern U.S., many of which are rare or even endangered.

Different habitats are represented along this trail—sunny wildflower meadow, Piedmont woodland, coastal plain, stream, bog, ridge, and southern Appalachian forest. Endless varieties of wildflowers blossoming from spring to fall can be enjoyed here.

Mountain Creek Lake Trail follows the water's edge through the woodlands and affords a view of a water community as well. **Wildflowers, rhododendrons,** and **native azaleas** are everywhere. During our summer visit, it was on this trail where we admired the most gorgeous specimens of native **plumleaf azalea** (*Rhododendron prunifolium*). Sit in a gazebo on the lakeshore and observe waterfowl, fish, and turtles. A walk on this trail is pleasant and relaxing.

Laurel Springs Trail is fairly rugged and follows the winding Laurel Springs Creek along the slopes of Pine Mountain Ridge. This area is quiet and secluded, an essentially undisturbed hardwood forest of oak and hickory. Thickets of **mountain laurel** (*Kalmia latifolia*) blossom usually in late April to early May. Interpretive signs are located along the trail, and don't forget to watch for Hollis quartzite stones used in the construction of Ida Cason Callaway Memorial Chapel and the country store.

The **Holly Trail**, not far from Mountain Creek Lake, is actually a group of trails that will lead you to explore not only native and quite unique **yellow Burford** and other **American holly** species, but also English and Oriental species as well. The collection of hollies here is considered the world's largest, amounting to well over 475 species and varieties. The variety you will see here will truly astound you: plants ranging from dwarfs to large trees, with berries ranging in color from red and orange to yellow and black. In the spring hollies provide the color with their blossoms. And again in the winter the hollies are not to be missed with their colorful berries that provide excellent bird food as well as many opportunities for winter bird watching. This is just another example of how a visit to the gardens in winter can be rewarding and enjoyable. **Camellias** bloom, and fragrances of **winter jasmine** (*Jasminum nudiflorum*) and **tea olive** (*Osmanthus fragrans*) permeate the air. And winter blooming **daphne** (*Daphne odora*), **winter honeysuckle** (*Lonicera fragrantissima*), and **wintersweet** (*Chimonanthus praecox*) add their fragrances as well. So keep in mind that winter is also the time to enjoy colors and fragrances of the gardens.

The **Cecil B. Day Butterfly Center,** which opened in 1988, is another attraction in Callaway Gardens that is in a league of its own. It encompasses 4.5 acres with an 8,000-square-foot rain forest conservatory enclosed in glass. An entryway building features educational displays and exhibits as well as beautiful artworks. There is a fascinating collection of butterfly watercolors by John Abbot from the period 1776 to 1840, and butterfly watercolors by nineteenth-century artist Chevalier de Freminville. Do not forget to visit the **Orientation Theater,** and see the twelve-minute award-winning film illuminating the life cycle of the butterfly. You will be better informed, and you will also appreciate much more what you will see when you enter the butterfly conservatory. The conservatory houses up to one thousand tropical butterflies and many species of tropical plants providing beauty and color for the visitors, but more importantly, providing everything needed for the life cycle of the butterfly.

Flowering plants contain nectar as a food source for adult butterflies, which will lay their eggs only on certain kind of plants, and once the eggs hatch, the larvae begin to feed on the host plant. But keep in mind that different species of butterflies prefer different species of flowers; the preference for a particular color of blossoms can change with the age of butterfly. The plant food sources for the caterpillars are not necessarily the same as those adult butterflies use as a source of nectar. So you see that a great deal of thought goes into creating a butterfly habitat. A multitude of specialized plants must be grown and precise climate conditions must be maintained to ensure the proper temperature and humidity levels ideal for both butterflies and tropical plants.

The **outdoor butterfly gardens,** covering about 1.5 acres, are designed with a special combination of plants allowing more than seventy native species of butterflies of this region to go through their life cycle in front of the eyes of visitors of this marvelous facility. Here, visitors can learn how to create their own butterfly garden. There are even scheduled workshops for home gardeners on planting butterfly gardens.

Mr. Cason's Vegetable Garden was started in 1960 and was the last major project of Cason J. Callaway before his death. He wanted to create a garden that would demonstrate and teach proper methods for growing fruits and vegetables, and he certainly succeeded in that. The result is a 7.5-acre garden, designed as three semicircular terraces, that produces more than four hundred varieties of crops.

Fresh produce is available for sale to visitors. There are not just edible fruit and vegetables here, but also herbs and flowers.

Probably the best known part of the vegetable garden is the **Home Demonstration Garden,** added in 1984, which also is the set for PBS television series—*Victory Garden South.* This garden, on the scale of a home garden, covers about one-fifth of an acre, and its flower and vegetable beds were designed for easy viewing. The large **Herb Garden** contains fragrant, culinary, and medicinal herbs. We also found here other uses for herbs: quite ingenious uses of **rosemary** as a landscaping tool beautifully trimmed into hedges, and plantings of **Mexican sage** to attract butterflies and hummingbirds. **Butterfly Garden** is planted with varieties of plants that attract butterflies. **All-America Test Garden** is a very important section of the vegetable garden, one of only a few such gardens in the South. Here, new varieties of vegetables and flowers are tested and judged as part of a selection process. Results then provide valuable information on how different varieties of plants perform in the region's climate. There are also wildflower test plots.

John A. Sibley Horticultural Center is one of the most advanced conservatory/garden complexes in the world. Opened in 1984, it raised the limits of conservatory design to a much higher level and utilized totally new design principles. According to one of the Callaway Gardens informational brochures: "The John A. Sibley Horticultural Center was founded on two unusual design principles. One was the expansion of the more traditional conservatory plantings to a broader concept of horticultural display. The other was the creation of a floral display that integrates indoor and outdoor settings. The Center's design produces a visual flow of garden areas from the inside to the outdoors and minimizes the visual impact of the actual structure."

The center covers five acres, with more than 20,000 square feet of indoor display areas and 30,000 square feet of production greenhouse space. Enjoy the following main sections of the center: the **Tropical Conservatory,** with its controlled environment, features plants native to tropical regions; the **Grotto,** just behind the waterfall, provides needed humidity for a variety of ferns; and the **Rock Wall Garden,** located along a winding, narrow path, lets you admire azaleas, camellias, and citrus. Adjacent is **James M. Sibley Sculpture Garden.** The **Floral Conservatory** will fascinate you with a variety of flowering plants. There are several major floral themes featured each year. The **Outdoor Garden,** with its shrub- and perennial-bordered lawns, offers pleasing green open space. There are various seasonal displays ranging from spring bulbs to fall chrysanthemums.

When you visit here and admire the beautiful displays, regardless of the season, you always feel comfortable, and from the look of the plants, they feel that way too. When you wander from one display to another, you don't even realize if you are inside or outside of this amazing structure. But that is how it was designed. And only when you stop yourself from enjoying flowers and colors and fragrances to pay close attention to construction elements of this facility, do you comprehend the amount of thought that went into its design. The building is oriented to the south, and during the summer the cooling is accomplished by the shade of deciduous trees planted along the south side, as well as by ventilation and cooling airflow created by building elevation. The misting system and moving water of the waterfall and pool lower the air temperature by evaporative cooling. During the winter, building elevation together with plant-ings along the north side help to deflect cold north winds, while the soil berm serves as insulation and also creates a south-facing slope inside. Glass blocks let the light in but stop the transfer of heat or cold. Deciduous trees on the south side, without their leaves, let in the maximum of sun. The heat from the sun radiation is stored in the rock walls and water of the pool during the day, and then is released at night. A radiant heat system supplements the natural energy when necessary.

How amazing to realize that visitors admiring the surrounding beauty are not even aware of any of the design marvels we have just mentioned. Just as it should be. This center is undoubtedly a combi-nation of architecture and horticulture at its best.

Better save plenty of time for Callaway Gardens, it is a uniquely beautiful place and there is so much to see.

Worth Seeing:
The **Ida Cason Callaway Memorial Chapel,** located by the Falls Creek Lake, was built to honor Cason J. Callaway's mother Ida. Completed in 1962 and dedicated by Dr. Norman Vincent Peale, the chapel is English Gothic, and almost all of the building materials are

from the Pine Mountain area or Georgia. The walls are of quartzite
fieldstone found nearby, and surrounding forests provided the red
oak beams. Boulders from the Pine Mountain area were used for the
sanctuary's stone altar, and north Georgia Cherokee flagstone was
used for the floor. Only the limestone arches and Vermont slate roof
are not native materials. Six stained-glass windows grace the chapel.
The north window represents a Piedmont hardwood forest; the south
window represents evergreen pines of the coastal plain. Four west
windows depict the seasons: the first shows the spring blossoms of
azaleas and dogwoods; the second features summer green leaves of
plumleaf azalea; the third shows the yellow, orange, and red colors of
fall; and the fourth highlights the hollies, ferns, and evergreens of
winter. Organ concerts are scheduled on a regular basis.

The **Pioneer Log Cabin,** dating back to the 1830s, was discovered in Troup County, Georgia, in 1959. After proper numbering of
all its pieces, the cabin was disassembled, transported to the gardens,
and reassembled at its present site. Furnishings and tools representative of the period were gathered to set up a complete demonstration
home and to show how previous generations lived.

Piedmont Region

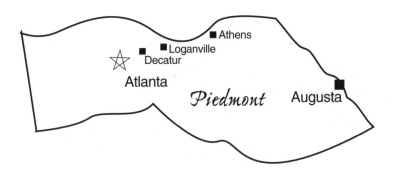

Old Government House

Blossoms of azaleas in the small front-yard garden proliferate with incredible color.

Address: 432 Telfair Street, Augusta, GA 30901
Directions: From I-20 take exit 66 and go east on GA 104 (River Watch Parkway) for about 4.8 miles. Make a left turn on Thirteenth Street and an immediate right turn onto Reynolds Street. Go for about a half mile and make a right turn onto Eighth Street. After about 0.3 miles make a left turn onto Telfair Street and go for about a half mile. The house will be on your right.
Hours: Grounds open daily from sunrise to sunset. The house is open Monday to Friday 9:00 a.m. to 5:00 p.m.
Closed: Saturday, Sunday, and holidays
Admission fee: no
Wheelchair access: yes
Facilities: none
Area: 1/4 acre
Phone: (706) 821-1812

Built in the American Federal style in 1801, the Old Government House was originally used as the municipal building for the city of Augusta as well as the county of Richmond. During the later years, the structure was used as a private residence, with appropriate modifications made to reflect the Greek Revival and Regency styles. Later years were not kind to this house, and the structure fell into a generalized state of disrepair. Remodeled and restored in the late 1980s, the property was finally saved.

The small front yard garden showcases magnificent **azaleas**. During our springtime visit, we could not take our eyes of them. Surrounded by **live oaks** and **southern magnolias** are the **dogwood trees** and **crape myrtles**. Do not miss the large **gingko tree** (*Gingko biloba*) believed to be the second largest in the United States, planted, as legend has it, for George Washington's visit in 1791. When you visit here and catch the peak of azaleas, all you can say is—unbelievable.

Pendleton King Park

Three separate gardens and an arboretum grace this beautiful Augusta park.

Address: Tree and Landscape Department, 1559 Eagles Way, Augusta, GA 30904

Directions: From I-20 take exit 66 and go on GA 104 (River Watch Parkway) for about 4.8 miles. Make a right turn onto Thirteenth Street and go through town on GA 4 for about three miles. Make a right turn onto Milledgeville Road and, after about 0.6 miles, make a right turn onto Kissingbower Road. After about one mile, the park entrance will be on your right.

Hours: 8:00 a.m. to 8:00 p.m. Monday to Saturday; 8:00 a.m. to 6:00 p.m. Sunday

Admission fee: no

Wheelchair access: yes

Facilities: none

Area: 64 acres

Phone: (706) 821-1670

A great deal of history goes with this largest of Augusta's public parks. In the early nineteenth century, John Pendleton King moved to Augusta to begin his illustrious career as a businessman. He was heavily involved in the building of the Augusta canal; he started and later on became president of the Georgia Railroad and Banking Company. He was also a brilliant lawyer and served in Washington as one of the country's youngest senators. This land, adjoining the lake (where the present park is located), is a part of what used to be Bugg Plantation. The property passed on to King's son, Henry Barkley King, born in 1844. He bequeathed this property for use as a bird sanctuary in memory of his only son, who died of pneumonia shortly after returning home from the First World War. The mansion standing on the property burned down in an accidental fire in 1916 and was never rebuilt. The property is still privately owned by the Henry B. King estate and is administered by its trustees. In 1972 the land was leased by the city of Augusta to be used as a park.

When we visited here in April, the spring blooms were at their best, and the **azaleas** could not look more spectacular. There are several areas to enjoy here. The formal garden, known as **The Sunken Blue Garden,** is more than one hundred years old. Surrounded by **red cedars, live oaks,** and **Southern magnolias,** it features only blue-blooming plants. We found **Touch and Smell Garden,** planted with herbs, quite intimate and delightful. **Walter A. Wilson Camellia Garden** and **Augusta Arboretum** are additional sections to enjoy. And when you don't want to explore anymore, just sit in one of the gazebos or on one of the numerous benches, relax, and just watch the scenery. We found Pendleton King Park quite an unexpected and very pleasant surprise.

Atlanta Botanical Garden

The Atlanta Botanical Garden is one of the premier botanical gardens in the nation. It offers thirty acres of beauty. Enjoy several display gardens. Diverse collections range from rare tropical plants in the spectacular Fuqua Conservatory to the Georgia native ferns and orchids in The Upper Woodlands.

Address: 1345 Piedmont Avenue NE, P.O. Box 77246, Atlanta, GA 30357

Directions: From I-85/75 take exit 101 and go east on Fourteenth Street until it dead-ends onto Piedmont Avenue NE. Make a left turn onto Piedmont Avenue NE, and after about a half mile, the garden entrance will be on your right.

Hours: October through February: Tuesday to Sunday 9:00 a.m. to 6:00 p.m. March through September: Tuesday to Sunday 9:00 a.m. to 7:00 p.m.

Closed: Mondays (except holidays), Thanksgiving, Christmas, and New Year's Day

Admission fee: yes

Wheelchair access: yes

Facilities: gift shop, café, Sheffield Botanical Library

Available: membership, guided tours, classes and lectures, symposia, and demonstrations

Area: 30 acres

Phone: (404) 876-5858 or (404) 876-5859

Right in the heart of midtown Atlanta, surrounded by the hustle and bustle of a vibrant city, is this refuge of peace and tranquility, a gem of a garden—the Atlanta Botanical Garden. It is hard to believe that as recently as the early 1970s there was not much of anything here, only an overgrown section of the city's historic Piedmont Park and an ambitious plan of a group of plant enthusiasts who very much wanted to create a botanical garden. And they made it happen; the Atlanta Botanical Garden was officially incorporated in 1976. Incorporation was just the beginning, then came an even bigger challenge—to actually create the garden. The hard work started with a skeleton staff aided by dedicated volunteers. It is also hard to believe that in those days the only structure at the garden was a trailer. From such humble beginnings, over a period of just twenty-plus years, we have witnessed the transformation of the fledgling Atlanta Botanical Garden into one of the premier botanical gardens in this country. Their mission is clear: "To develop and maintain plant collections for the purpose of display, education, research, conservation, and enjoyment."

The entire garden encompasses thirty acres, fifteen acres of display gardens and fifteen acres of natural woodland. Let's explore the display gardens first.

The **Japanese Garden** actually predates the founding of the Atlanta Botanical Garden. Originally established by the Atlanta Bonsai Society in 1960, the garden was renovated to its present appearance in 1980. It features the traditional elements of Japanese garden design. **Bamboo** represents resilience against adversity, stone or **pine** symbolizes longevity, and **blossoming trees** stand for youth and renewal.

The Atlanta Botanical Garden's **Rose Garden** dates back to the 1960s. The Greater Atlanta Rose Society planted and maintained a rose garden on this site. After complete renovation in 1990 it became an **All-America Display Garden**. More than one hundred varieties of roses are displayed here.

The **Herb Garden** was one of the first display gardens created in the Atlanta Botanical Garden. Walled in as is customary, it has a boxwood-edged, traditional English knot garden in its center. Borders feature perennial and annual herbs used for culinary, medicinal, and fragrance purposes. Wide varieties of herbs that are popular and thrive in the Piedmont region are showcased.

The **Vine Arbor** that runs along the conservatory greenhouses exhibits a very respectable collection of flowering vines, native and exotic, evergreen and deciduous, that are hardy and suitable for the Southeast.

The **Dwarf Conifer Garden,** situated in front of the Fuqua Conservatory, features more than two hundred varieties of dwarf, rare, and unusual conifers. Conifers from all over the world are represented, including over thirty varieties of **Japanese cedar**.

Dorothy Chapman Fuqua Conservatory is a magnificent, state-of-the-art, 23,000-square-foot structure that was opened to the public in March 1989. When you enter, you really step into another

world. It is a true botanical paradise and home to more than seven thousand tropical and desert plants from around the world, many of them rare or endangered. Enjoy collections of exotic tropical plants: **ferns, bromeliads, palms**, and **cycads**. The collection of **orchids** boasts well over one thousand. Epiphytic and terrestrial species as well as hybrid orchids thrive here. As they come into bloom, orchids are rotated from the greenhouses to the conservatory for visitors to enjoy. **Waterfall Display** area in the rotunda is reserved to show off species orchids. In the rotunda, which is the main portion of the conservatory, a humid, misty Amazonian rain forest environment is recreated, complete with colorful amphibians and free-flying birds.

A different plant environment has to be maintained in the other part of the conservatory—the **Desert House**. Here, in a faithfully recreated desert environment, **succulents** mostly from the Old World are displayed. These plants have evolved to develop special water storage capabilities in order to survive during long periods of drought. The collection showcases several large families of succulent plants, placing major emphasis on plants from the island of Madagascar. **Orangerie** is another interesting part of the conservatory. Originally, old European orangeries provided fresh citrus during the winter months. In addition to **citrus** the Orangerie in Fuqua Conservatory displays a variety of **tropical fruits, nuts,** and **spices**.

The environment in all parts of the conservatory as well as in the support greenhouses is carefully monitored. Temperature, humidity, shade, and air circulation can be controlled and adjusted as necessary. The sophisticated computer system keeps all the necessary parameters in optimal ranges, true masterpiece of technology.

The **Carnivorous Plant Bog,** located behind the Fuqua Conservatory, is planted with hardy carnivorous plants. These plants have evolved in nutrient-poor areas of wetlands; they therefore depend on animal prey, rather than nutrients from the soil, to survive. They have adapted extremely well to their environment and developed the ability to trap and digest insects. There are several ways these plants manage to catch their meal. In the case of **Venus flytrap** (*Dionaea muscipula*), the plant closes around its prey as soon as the insect brushes against its fine trigger hairs. **Pitcher plants** in the genus *Sarracenia* attract insects with the allure of their colors and the fragrance of their nectars. Its leaves are modified into pitcher-shaped, hollow receptacles, allowing it to hold liquid. As soon as an insect slides inside the pitcher, there is no way to escape up its slippery walls, and enzymes will do the rest, dissolving the prey completely. The **sundews,** a common name for the genus *Drosera,* have their hairy leaves covered with a sticky substance that will catch the insect. **Butterwort** is a common name for the species of *Pinguicula*. The greasy-looking surface of their leaves is covered with soft hairs secreting a sticky substance that catches small insects. Once the insect is caught, the edges of the leaf roll over, retaining the insect, which is later digested.

Since many carnivorous plants are endangered primarily because of their habitat destruction, the Atlanta Botanical Garden is actively involved in the restoration of critical habitats as well as greenhouse propagation of the **purple pitcher plant** (*Sarracenia purpurea*).

There is so much more to see: **Rock Garden, Vegetable Garden/Orchard, Fragrance Garden, Summer Bulb Collection, Perennial Borders, Hardy Cacti and Succulents, Iris Garden, Hardy Palms,** and much more.

The fifteen acres of natural woodland, the **Storza Woods,** is one of the last remaining tracts of hardwood forest that remains in the city of Atlanta. It offers a diverse habitat for plant and animal life. There is a 1.25-mile interpretive **nature trail** that winds its way through the woodlands.

The **Upper Woodland,** covering approximately five acres, is primarily devoted to shade plants. **Fern Glade** features native

Georgia ferns, from the large **cinnamon fern** to the delicate **maidenhair fern**. Many of Georgia's native species of orchids are displayed in this area. Then there are **Wildflower Garden, Woodland Rockery,** and **Backyard Wildlife Habitat** to see. The **Camellia Collection** features a hardy combination of cultivars blooming from November to February.

At the time of this writing, the new, two-acre **Egleston Scottish Rite Children's Health Care System Children's Garden** was just about to open.

The Atlanta Botanical Garden displays its beautiful collections, but it does much more than that. The garden's horticulture staff is involved in several conservation projects aimed to preserve endangered native plants. They are involved in habitat restorations and plant rescues, so plants can be propagated and reintroduced into the wild. Atlanta Botanical Garden is an integral part of the community and is working tirelessly to educate the public about the importance of conservation. That is the key; only education will make us realize that we must behave responsibly and stop the habitat destruction and the loss of biodiversity. From schoolchildren to adults, everyone is introduced to nature, plants, and conservation. There are many ways to educate, from informal guided walks through the garden all the way up to the University of Georgia Lecture Series. Classes, lectures, workshops, and symposia cover a wide variety of topics. Atlanta Botanical Garden is also the hub for many plant societies.

The **plantmobile** is a very important and immensely popular outreach program. It is a garden on wheels that takes horticultural programs and unusual plants to schools and community centers. And if you are a gardener having problems with one of your plants, do not despair. Just call the garden's **Plant Hotline** and one of the experts will answer your questions or dispense advice. What else can we say?—a beautiful garden, a special place to visit.

Atlanta History Center

Right in the middle of Atlanta is this thirty-three-acre complex of gardens, historic houses, and a museum. Plenty to enjoy and plenty to learn.

Address: 130 West Paces Ferry Road NW, Atlanta, GA 30305

Directions: From I-75 take exit 107 for West Paces Ferry Road. The exit ramp will get you onto Northside Parkway. At the next traffic light make a right turn onto West Paces Ferry Road. Follow the signs, and after about three miles, you will see the Atlanta History Center on your right.

Hours: 10:00 a.m. to 5:30 p.m. Monday through Saturday; 12:00 p.m. to 5:30 p.m. Sunday

Closed: Thanksgiving, Christmas and New Year's Day. Holiday hours may vary.

Admission fee: yes

Wheelchair access: yes

Facilities: library, café, restaurant, and gift shop

Available: membership, lectures, educational programs, group rates

Area: 33 acres

Phone: (404) 814-4000

Starting in 1966, the Atlanta Historical Society embarked on a path of preservation and acquired the Swan House and ten acres of surrounding gardens. The rest, as they say, is history. Today, this thirty-three-acre complex of several gardens and buildings provides an oasis of beauty and learning, right in the middle of Atlanta, just a few minutes from downtown. Walk through the gardens, follow the nature trails through the woodlands, and discover the horticultural history of the Atlanta region.

Beautiful formal gardens featuring a terraced front lawn and boxwood garden surround the **Swan House,** the elegant residence for which Palazzo Corsini in Rome was the inspiration. Enjoy the classical statuary, fountains, cascades, and formal vistas.

From here, follow **Swan Woods Trail,** the delightful woodland trail winding its way through a ten-acre forest of **oaks, pines, beeches,** and **hickories**. Interpretive markers will guide you

through this woodland ecosystem. The **Garden for Peace** is located on the Swan Woods Trail. It features "The Peace Tree," a fourteen-foot sculpture by Georgi Japaridze, a sculptor from Atlanta's Russian sister city of Tbilisi. The Gardens for Peace are an international network of gardens founded in 1984 by Atlanta native Laura Dorsey Rains. The marker in the Garden for Peace says it best: "Promoting peace in the world through the universal language of gardens." The first garden in the Gardens for Peace international network was dedicated at the Atlanta History Center in April 1988, with the second one in Tbilisi in May 1988.

The **Frank A. Smith Memorial Rhododendron Garden** features hundreds of varieties of **rhododendrons** and **azaleas** that seem to thrive under the dense forest canopy.

The **Cherry Sims Asian American Garden** highlights important Asian plant species and their southeastern American counterparts. Many cultivars of **Japanese maples** are represented here.

Plantings around the **Tullie Smith Farm** feature period **herbs** and **vegetables**.

And what a pleasant surprise the **Mary Howard Gilbert Memorial Quarry Garden** is. Just imagine that rock from this three-acre quarry was used to build many local roads during the last century and even the early part of this one. Actually, quarrying only stopped around 1920. In 1976 this garden was dedicated in honor of the founding members of the **Mimosa Garden Club,** who reclaimed and planted this garden. We found this garden especially enjoyable. Follow the wooden and mulch walkways over the footbridges, feast on wildflowers and ferns. **Sycamore trees** (*Platanus occidentalis*) and **sweet bays** (*Magnolia virginiana*) provide shade, and there are native plants everywhere. And yes, you are still in the middle of Atlanta.

Worth Seeing:

Tour the **Swan House,** named for the swan motif featured
throughout the interior of the house. It was designed in Classical
style by Atlanta architect Phillip Trammell Shutze and completed in
1928 for Edward Hamilton Inman, an heir to a cotton brokerage
fortune. Shutze was a well-known architect who designed several
other Atlanta landmark buildings. The Atlanta History Center
acquired Swan House and most of its furnishings in 1966. Phillip
Trammell Shutze bequeathed his personal collection of decorative
arts and his research library to the Atlanta History Center in 1982.
Rotating selections from this extensive collection are exhibited in the
Swan House. This well-known Atlanta landmark is listed on the
National Register of Historic Places.

Tullie Smith House and Farm, home to the Smith family until
1967, was built in the 1840s.

It was originally located a few miles east of Atlanta, and this was
probably the reason it survived the nearly complete destruction of
Atlanta in 1864. The entire farm complex was moved to the Atlanta
History Center site in 1972. The complex includes a farmhouse,
detached kitchen, and outbuildings. Everyday activities typical of
rural mid-1800s Georgia are demonstrated here. The house features
furniture and objects typical of the period, and is listed on the
National Register of Historic Places.

McElreath Hall houses a library and archives, completed in
1975, containing more than 3.5 million items available for research.
It includes books, prints, photographs, drawings, postcards, public
records, and maps.

Atlanta History Museum, opened in 1993, is one of the
country's largest history museums. It features the award-winning
Civil War exhibit "Turning Point: The American Civil War"; an
exhibit offering a comprehensive view of Atlanta's history, "Metro-
politan Frontiers: Atlanta, 1835–2000"; and a Southern folk arts
exhibit. Several changing exhibitions and special events take place
here as well.

Cator Woolford Gardens

*Beautiful six-acre gardens in the Druid Hills section of Atlanta
are surrounded by a virgin forest of hickory, beech, and pine.*

Address: 1815 Ponce de Leon Avenue, NW, Atlanta, GA 30307
Directions: From I-85/75 take exit 100 to North Street and go east
for about 0.4 miles. Make a left turn onto Piedmont Avenue NE
and at the next traffic light make a right turn onto Ponce de Leon
Avenue NE. Go for about three miles. Make a right turn onto
Clifton Road NE and then an immediate left turn onto South
Ponce de Leon Avenue NE. Very shortly you will see the garden
gate on your right.
Hours: Open daily from sunrise to sunset
Admission fee: no
Wheelchair access: yes
Facilities: none
Area: 6 acres
Phone: (404) 377-3836

In the Druid Hills section of Atlanta, Cator Woolford Gardens is
located on what once was Jacqueland, the thirty-three-acre estate
of the gardens' namesake, Cator Woolford, founder and president
of the Retail Credit
Company. In 1921 he
commissioned a Philadel-
phia landscape architect
to design the gardens.
Woolford passed on
in 1944, and the
estate was
purchased by the
Children Reha-
bilitation
Center in
1949. The
gardens

were restored in Cator Woolford's memory by his relatives and friends for the cerebral palsy center.

A virgin forest of **hickories, beeches,** and **pines** surrounds the gardens. Two symmetrical pergolas flank the central lawn. There are **Perennial Garden, Bog Garden, Rock Garden,** and **Wildflower Bog** to see. And do not forget to walk the winding and very peaceful **Woodland Trail**. During the early spring the **azaleas, dogwoods,** and **flowering trees** steal the show; later on **rhododendrons** and **roses** take center stage. Mature **Southern magnolias, crape myrtles, holies,** and **camellias** grace the gardens, and flower borders add an additional color accent. With the wide variety of plantings there is always some pleasant surprise waiting here, regardless of the season.

Fernbank Science Center

Amazing and unique complex of museums, gardens, forest, and classrooms dedicated to education and science. Fernbank Forest is a sixty-five-acre tract of undisturbed hardwood forest in the middle of Atlanta, with a rose garden containing over 1,300 roses.

Address: 156 Heaton Park Drive NE, Atlanta, GA 30307

Directions: From I-75/85 take exit 100 and go east for about 0.4 miles. Make a left turn onto Piedmont Avenue NE. Make a right turn at the next traffic light onto Ponce de Leon Avenue NE. After about four miles make a left turn onto Artwood Road; after about 0.2 miles turn right onto Heaton Park Drive.

Hours: 8:30 a.m. to 5:00 p.m. Monday; 8:30 a.m. to 10:00 p.m. Tuesday to Friday; 10:00 a.m. to 5:00 p.m. Saturday; 1:00 p.m. to 5:00 p.m. Sunday

Admission fee: no

Wheelchair access: yes

Facilities: natural history exhibits, agricultural demonstrations, one of the largest planetariums in the country

Area: 65 acres

Phone: (404) 378-4311

From its inception, the Fernbank Science Center has remained dedicated to education, science, and preservation. Fernbank Forest was purchased in 1937 from Colonel Z. D. Harrison by a group of citizens interested in preserving this forest for science and education. In 1964 the DeKalb County Board of Education accepted the forty-eight-year lease proposed by the Fernbank Board of Trustees. The lease stipulated that the forest is to be used by all citizens of the state and the region, that it be maintained and protected in as near natural state as possible, that the forest be fenced, that all entry and use be controlled, and that no plants or animals are to be removed. The lease is reviewed yearly and is renewed at eight-year intervals. The Fernbank Science Center building was completed and dedicated in 1967, and the spectacular Fernbank Museum of Natural History opened in 1992.

The center promotes scientifical educational activities on all levels, including ongoing programs for the DeKalb School System from preschool through adult education.

Your visit begins in the Fernbank Science Center building, and as you emerge outside, do not miss **Vegetable Garden, Herb Garden, Bog,** and **Butterfly and Hummingbird Gardens** located just behind the main center building. The **Home Composting Demonstration Site** is also here. Several different species of plants used in landscaping can also be viewed in this area. All the plants are properly labeled with common and Latin names. From here, you head straight for Fernbank Forest.

Fernbank Forest

This sixty-five-acre tract of undisturbed oak, hickory, and beech forest in essentially primeval condition is unique in the Piedmont region. It is amazing that this forest just happens to be in the middle of Atlanta. This forest is the heart of the center; it also is a "living laboratory" or "school in the woods" if you prefer. That is why during school hours students are here to study biology, botany, and horticulture. The general public can enjoy this forest in the afternoons and on weekends. There are 1.5 miles of paved trails to enjoy, with **trees, shrubs, wildflowers,** and **ferns** nicely labeled, so they can be readily identified. Seasonal guidesheets emphasize wildflowers, forest ecology, or tree identification. An **Easy Effort Trail** is available for individuals with physical disabilities. Braille recorders and taped narration are available, and a section of trail has been outfitted with guide ropes to help the visually impaired. And while you are exploring Fernbank Forest, don't miss the **Elephant Rock,** or a subterranean window which allows you to observe aquatic life of a small pond from below the ground level.

Robert L. Staton Rose Garden

Address: 767 Clifton Road NE, Atlanta, GA 30307
Directions: From I-75/85 take exit 100 and go east on North Street for about 0.4 miles. Make a left turn onto Piedmont Avenue NE, and at the next traffic light right turn onto Ponce de Leon

Avenue NE and go for about three miles. Make a left turn onto Clifton Road NE. After about 0.2 miles the entrance will be on your right.

Hours: Open daily from sunrise to sunset
Admission fee: no
Wheelchair access: yes
Facilities: none
Area: 1 acre
Phone: (404) 378-4311

Located on the beautiful grounds of the Fernbank Museum of Natural History, this garden is named in honor of Robert L. Staton, who established a rose garden at Fernbank. A rose enthusiast since childhood, Staton was a horticulturist who truly had a lifelong love affair with roses. He developed the proposal that became the foundation of the rose garden, which was established in 1983.

More than 1,300 **roses** thrive here, and this garden has the distinction of being one of only three gardens in the United States with both ARS (American Rose Society) Award of Excellence miniature test roses and AARS (All American Rose Selection) test roses. The garden also contains donated named roses. You can admire beautiful blossoms, colors, and fragrances from May until the winter frost.

Briarcliff Greenhouses

Address: 1256 Briarcliff Road, Atlanta, GA 30306
Directions: From I-75/85 take exit 100 and go east for about 0.4 miles. Make a left turn onto Piedmont Avenue NE, and then a right turn at the next traffic light onto Ponce de Leon Avenue NE. Continue on Ponce de Leon Avenue for about two miles. Make a left turn onto Briarcliff Road, and soon the greenhouses will be on your left.
Hours: Sunday 1:00 p.m. to 5:00 p.m. only
Admission fee: no
Wheelchair access: yes
Facilities: none
Phone: (404) 378-4311

This property known as "Briarcliff" was the mansion of Asa G. Candler Jr., son of the founder of the Coca-Cola Company. The original structure was built in 1912, and the present mansion was completed in 1920. The **Lord and Burnham Victorian greenhouses** were constructed in 1920 and renovated in 1988. The botanical collections of the Fernbank Science Center were moved into the greenhouses in 1989. In 1998 Emory University purchased this property, which is on the National Register of Historic Places.

DeKalb County students come here to learn about a variety of plant-related topics. Students even get hands-on experience—they will plant the seed, make a cutting, or take a seedling to care for at home. There is a classroom right here in the greenhouse, and even an observational beehive. Because the greenhouses are used for teaching they are open to the public on Sunday afternoons only. The atrium contains large specimens such as **palms, staghorn ferns,** and **citrus**. In other sections you will find a variety of plants: **cacti** and **succulents, ferns, begonias, orchids,** and **bromeliads**. Don't forget to see the plantings and flowerbeds outside of the greenhouses. A horticulturist will answer any questions you may have and, upon completion of your visit, you even get a free small plant to take home with you.

Fernbank complex is a unique place that offers learning in an innovative and enjoyable way.

Worth Seeing:

The **Fernbank Planetarium** is one of the largest in the United States. The planetarium theater's dome, which also serves as a projection screen, has a seventy-foot diameter. The Carl Zeiss Mark V planetarium projector contains two hundred separate projectors capable of reproducing a sky containing the sun, moon, visible planets, and nine thousand stars. Two hundred and fifty additional projectors are available for special effects. It's simply amazing.

The **Exhibit Hall** features permanent as well as changing exhibits that illustrate the natural environment and vanishing habitats of Georgia and the Southeast from prehistory to the present time.

The **Fairbank Observatory** houses the largest telescope in the southeastern United States. It is composed of a thirty-six-inch Cassegrain reflector on a fork equatorial mount. It is the largest telescope in the world that is dedicated primarily to public education.

The **Fernbank Museum of Natural History** features as permanent exhibits "A Walk Through Time in Georgia," "Cultures of the World," "Spectrum of the Senses," "World of Shells," and "Children's Discovery Rooms."

Chatham County Garden Center and Botanical Gardens
Savannah

Old Government House
Augusta

Pebble Hill Plantation
Thomasville

Vines Botanical Gardens
Loganville

Pendleton King Park
Augusta

State Botanical Garden of Georgia
Athens

Founders Memorial Garden
Athens

Oak Hill and the Martha Berry Museum
Mount Berry

Guido Gardens
Metter

Callaway Gardens
Pine Mountain

The Crescent
Valdosta

Atlanta Botanical Garden
Atlanta

Mr. Cason's Vegetable Garden, Callaway Gardens
Pine Mountain

Lockerly Arboretum
Milledgeville

Barnsley Gardens
Adairsville

Antique Rose Emporium
Dahlonega

Founders Memorial Garden
Athens

William Scarbrough House
Savannah

Andrew Low House
Savannah

Cator Woolford Gardens
Atlanta

Atlanta History Center
Atlanta

DeKalb College Botanical Gardens

This small, recently planted garden is a refuge for native hard-to-find and hard-to-grow plants as well as plants that are threatened or endangered.

Address: 3251 Panthersville Road, Decatur, GA 30034
Directions: From I-285 take exit 36 and go east on Flat Shoals
    Parkway (GA 155) for about 0.5 miles. Turn right onto Clifton
    Springs Road, go 0.6 miles, and then turn left onto Panthersville
    Road. The gardens parking area will be on your right.
Hours: Open daily from sunrise to sunset
Admission fee: no
Wheelchair access: partial
Facilities: none
Area: 4 acres
Phone: (404) 244-5052

This garden is quite young as gardens go, started in just 1990 by the students of DeKalb College. The garden is dedicated to the propagation and preservation of indigenous plants and is administered jointly by DeKalb College and DeKalb County. It is an outdoor classroom for the students and horticulture enthusiasts. The garden's emphasis is on native hard-to-find and hard-to-grow plants, and many plants here are rare, threatened, or endangered. It is already the largest native plant garden in Georgia. With over twelve hundred plant species at the present time, its goal is to have over two thousand plant species represented.

When exploring the gardens you will find interesting plantings everywhere. During our early spring visit we admired the blossoms of **Piedmont azalea** (*Rhododendron canescens*) and **Florida azalea** (*Rhododendron austrinum*). Follow the trail to the lower sections of gardens, where in the wet areas near the creek we found a very respectable collection of ferns under the canopy of mostly pines. Several endangered, smaller **needle palms** (*Rhapidophyllum hystrix*) were thriving here. Then there are beds of **irises,** the colorful **Perennial Garden,** and even raised beds with a multitude of plants to enjoy. And we are confident that with the passage of time, as the garden matures, it will just get better and better.

Vines Botanical Gardens

Twenty-five acres of elaborate gardens surround a sun-glittered lake. Distinctive theme gardens and antique statuary lend grace and beauty.

Address: 3500 Oak Grove Road, Loganville, GA 30052

Directions: From I-285 take exit 30B and go east on US 78 through Stone Mountain and Snelville until you get to Loganville. Watch for an Exxon station on your left side, and just after you pass it make a left turn onto Brand Street, then an immediate left turn onto Oak Grove Road. Continue on Oak Grove Road for about 1.8 miles; the entrance to the gardens will be on your right.

Hours: 10:00 a.m. to 5:00 p.m. Tuesday to Sunday

Closed: Mondays

Admission fee: yes

Wheelchair access: almost complete

Facilities: gift shop, restaurant, and botanical research library

Available: membership, classes, demonstrations and special events, guided tours by prior appointment

Area: 25 acres

Phone: (770) 466-7532

Located east of Atlanta in quiet Gwinnett County, within sight of Stone Mountain, Vines Botanical Gardens was, in the late 1970s, the estate of Charles and Myrna Adams. The Adams greatly improved the property and the twenty-five acres of elaborate gardens. They lived on the property until 1990, when they donated the estate to Gwinnett County in memory of Mrs. Adams' father, Oldie Vines. The county's parks and recreation department led the transformation from a private to a public garden. In 1994, the gardens were turned over to the Vines Botanical Gardens Foundation, Inc., a private, nonprofit organization, to run the gardens. In 1997 the gardens were privatized again. An adequate amount of money was pledged by the new owners towards major renovations that will ensure that Vines Botanical Gardens will continue to serve the county not only as a public garden but also as an educational and special-event facility.

As you enter, you will immediately see that gardens surround the 3.5-acre lake that is home to swans, geese, and ducks. White wooden footbridges cross the lake, and gazebos offer shelter from the sun or a place from  which to watch the lake or fountains. As you begin to stroll around, pathways will lead you through distinctive theme gardens with abundant and diverse plantings. Antique statuary incorporated into the design accents the gardens.

Follow the boardwalk through the **Asian Garden** under the canopy of **tall pines,** surrounded by **rhododendrons** and **Japanese maples**. **Rose Colonade Garden** showcases a large collection of over eighty varieties of **antique roses,** labeled not just by their names, but also by the year of introduction. Statues depicting four seasons of the year highlight the garden. The adjoining **White Garden** surrounding the gazebo features plant varieties selected for their white flowers or variegated foliage. The **Oldie Vines Flower Garden** displays a spectrum of colors and textures throughout the year. This garden is dedicated to the joy of flower gardening.

Woodland Terrace showcases fifty different varieties of **hostas**. *Hosta spp.* (**Plantain lilies**) are low-growing, clump-forming perennials, grown mostly for their attractive, large, and ribbed foliage, which you can admire from spring to fall. Plans call for enlarging this collection to over three hundred varieties. Don't forget to see the **Whimsical Garden, Southscape Garden,** and the **Reflection Pool**.

State Botanical Garden of Georgia

This 313-acre garden showcases several outdoor theme gardens and special collections, has a large conservatory for subtropical and tropical plants, and offers miles of nature trails. There is so much to see, better reserve at least a half day.

Address: 2450 South Milledge Avenue, Athens, GA 30605

Directions: From I-20 take exit 51 and go north on US 441 for about twenty-nine miles. Make a right turn onto South Milledge Avenue, and after about one mile the garden entrance will be on your right. From I-85 take exit 53 and go south on US 441 south for about twenty miles. Then take the GA 10 loop for about six miles to the South Milledge Avenue exit. Continue south on Milledge Avenue for about one mile, and the garden entrance will be on your right.

Hours: October to March: open daily from 8:00 a.m. to 6:00 p.m. April to September: 8:00 a.m. to 8:00 p.m. The Visitor Center/Conservatory is open 9:00 a.m. to 4:30 p.m. Monday to Saturday; 11:30 a.m. to 4:30 p.m. Sunday.

Closed: major holidays

Admission fee: no, donations appreciated

Wheelchair access: partial

Facilities: visitor center, chapel, gift shop, café, Callaway Building

Available: membership, lectures, workshops, special events

Area: 313 acres

Phone: (706) 542-1244

Located just outside of Athens, about three miles from the University of Georgia campus, is the sprawling and beautiful State Botanical Garden of Georgia. The garden was founded as the University of Georgia Botanical Garden in 1968 when the University of Georgia set aside a 293-acre tract of land. In 1984 the garden was renamed the State Botanical Garden of Georgia to more accurately reflect its role in statewide education and research. The Garden serves as a repository for special collections, including native flora, commercially important cultivars, and rare and endangered species.

The garden grew further in 1990, when a private donation of twenty adjacent acres near the Middle Oconee River brought the total acreage to 313.

Why not start your visit in the **Visitor Center,** a beautiful glass structure completed in 1984. Here visitors can pick up a map of the garden or view an orientation program in the theater area. And in the foyer of the Visitor Center one can see changing art exhibitions featuring horticultural, botanical, and conservation themes. The building also houses a three-story, 10,000-square-foot **Conservatory** featuring a permanent collection of subtropical and tropical plants. Many of the species, especially from tropical rainforests, are now endangered.

And once you step outside of the Visitor Center, with the map of the garden firmly in your hand, just look how many special collections there are to see.

The three-acre **International Garden** adjacent to the Visitor Center is one of the newer horticultural additions. The garden is highly interpretive and tells of the relationship between people and plants over the ages. Three eras that greatly influenced the evolution of botanical gardens are represented here: the Middle Ages, the Age of Exploration, and the Age of Conservation. Representing the Middle Ages are the **Herb Garden,** which displays herbs used mainly for culinary and fragrance purposes, and the **Physic Garden,** which features medicinal herbs. The Age of Exploration was the era of the worldwide search for new, useful, or valuable plants. This was also an era of growth for botanical gardens as places to introduce and study the new discoveries. Different sections representing the geographic areas from which the plants originated are featured. And the Age of Conservation is interpreted through the **Threatened and Endangered Plants** section, the **American Indian Plants** section, and the **Bog Garden**. We are reminded that conservation must be on our minds and also in our actions to prevent the continuing habitat destruction and the alarming loss of biodiversity. Altogether, there are eleven horticultural and botanical collections here, not just interesting and informative, but also quite thought provoking.

The **Shade Garden** features seven sections of shade-loving species, honoring the seven districts of the Garden Club of Georgia, a major donor in the 1988 renovation of the garden. The districts—**Azalea, Camellia, Dogwood, Laurel, Magnolia, Oleander,** and

Redbud—all feature plants of the same name. The only exception is the Oleander. Oleanders are not hardy enough for the Athens area, so **viburnums** were chosen as alternates. During our spring visit the profusion of blossoms of **wisteria** (*Wisteria sinensis*) covering the arbor was spectacular. Standing under the arbor, enjoying the intoxicating fragrance of wisteria, was quite a noisy affair as literally hundreds of bumblebees were enjoying and working the wisteria as well. The blossoms of the surrounding **dogwood trees** (*Cornus florida*) and **redbud trees** (*Cercis canadensis*) were just amazing in the soft, filtered light.

The native azalea collection, featuring deciduous species and hybrids, can be found in the **Galle Native Azalea Garden**. In 1987 it was dedicated in honor of Fred C. Galle, a well-known azalea expert and the author of *Azaleas,* which is a respected and recognized reference on the subject.

The **Rhododendron Garden** was established in 1976 through the gift of the Athens Garden Club. Here, mostly hybrid rhododendrons show off their conspicuous blossoms in a wide spectrum of colors in late spring. The hybrid rhododendrons are more suitable for this area, since the native rhododendrons, quite common in north

Georgia, do not usually do well as far south and east as Athens.

The **Rose Garden,** established in 1975, is an official All-America Rose Garden. It features all major classes of modern roses as well as several antique roses. Georgia's state flower, **Cherokee rose** (*Rosa laevigata*), can be enjoyed here as well.

The **Native Flora Garden** contains more than three hundred species native to Georgia and the southeastern United States. Many of the species featured here are rare, threatened, or endangered.

The **Annual/Perennial Garden** is probably the most colorful section of the State Botanical Garden of Georgia. The **All-America Selections Display Garden** is probably at its best when the summer annuals peak, but the variety of colors and textures provides plenty to see throughout the year. Plants attracting butterflies and hummingbirds are here too. In an adjacent area, flowers for drying provide materials for workshops on dried flower crafts. An area nearby is devoted to children's gardening.

The **Groundcover Collection** features a variety of groundcovers that are appropriate for use in the Southeast. Groundcovers in general offer alternatives to turf; many of them also flower, thus adding color to the landscape, not to mention their usefulness in preventing soil erosion.

The **Dahlia Garden** was dedicated in 1987 and features several varieties that represent many of the dahlia's classes and colors. Native to Central and South America, dahlias have been extensively hybridized and grown around the world. Twelve classes of dahlias, based on flower morphology with the entire color spectrum represented, are recognized by the American Dahlia Society. The unquestionable star of this garden is the **Piedmont rebel**, a dahlia variety that grows to the height of four feet with red flowers measuring up to eight inches across.

The **Trial Garden** represents a unique section of the garden. Here, varieties of plants are evaluated and assessed for their appearance, hardiness, landscape potential, disease and insect resistance, and other parameters. Many of them are introduced species, and the purpose is to evaluate their adaptability to the southeastern United States. After a few years, depending on the outcome, the plants are propagated, transplanted to a permanent location, or eliminated.

The garden embraces many topics: education, research, plant conservation, and habitat protection, just to name a few. But education is without question the garden's highest goal. The garden truly is a "living laboratory" for university teaching and research. University students and faculty utilize the garden's collections in a variety of courses and studies. And on top of that, each year the State Botanical Garden of Georgia offers at least eighty educational programs and events. They include courses, lectures, and workshops on topics covering botany, horticulture, gardening, and a whole spectrum of related topics.

There are also five miles of color-coded **Nature Trails** winding through the garden. The **White Trail** is the longest and stretches from the Middle Oconee River to the upland hardwood forest. The **Red, Green, Blue, Purple,** and **Yellow** are shorter trails, acting as connecting segments. As you walk the trails, you can observe plant communities found in various ecological areas of the garden, ranging from wetlands and floodplains to slopes and uplands. **Birdwatching** is quite popular in the garden, and several species of birds are in their natural habitat here. The Georgia Ornithological Society adopted the **Orange Trail,** leading through the eastern section of the garden, paralleling the Middle Oconee River for several hundred yards.

Worth Seeing: Take a tour of the **Day Chapel**. The chapel, completed in 1994, was given by the family of Cecil B. Day Sr. in his memory. Located in a secluded area of a hardwood forest, the chapel is modern in design and contains an eclectic blend of architectural styles and details. The building, constructed mostly of native cypress and stone, is set on a Belgian block foundation. The Belgian blocks came from Atlanta, where they were originally used to pave Decatur Street. Many unique decorative elements are used here. The imposing door of carved mahogany and glass that leads into the sanctuary incorporates into its design the state tree (live oak), state bird (brown thrasher), state butterfly (Eastern yellow swallowtail), and state flower (Cherokee rose).

Founders Memorial Garden

Small but intimate, the garden features formal and informal arrangements that delight the eye with stained-glass brilliance.

Address: The Garden Club of Georgia, Inc., 325 South Lumpkin Street, Athens, GA 30602

Directions: From I-20 take exit 51 and go north on US 441 for about twenty-nine miles. Make a left turn onto South Milledge Avenue, and go north for about 2.5 miles. Make a right turn onto Broad Street, and continue for about 1.7 miles. Make a right turn onto South Lumpkin Street, and shortly the garden will be on your left. From I-85 take exit 53 and go south on US 441 for about twenty miles. Then take GA 10 and after six miles look for the South Milledge Avenue exit. Go north on South Milledge Avenue for about 1.1 miles, then make a right turn onto South Lumpkin Street. After about 1.5 miles the garden will be on your right.

Hours: The garden is open daily, sunrise to sunset. The museum house is open for tours by appointment. The office is open 9:00 a.m. to noon and 1:00 p.m. to 4:00 p.m. Monday through Friday. Closed on Saturday, Sunday, and most major holidays.

Admission fee: donations accepted

Wheelchair access: partial

Facilities: none

Area: 2.5 acres

Phone: (706) 542-3631

This garden commemorates the founding of the first garden club in the nation. In 1891 twelve women organized and founded the Ladies' Garden Club of Athens, which later became the nation's first garden club. In 1936 the state garden club wanted to create a fitting memorial to the founders; a fund was established to create a living monument, a garden that would be located on the University of Georgia campus. Design and development of the garden proceeded under the direction of Hubert Owens, who was the head of the University of Georgia's Department of Landscape Architecture at that time. After ten years of work, the garden was completed in 1946. The garden surrounds the 1857 Lumpkin House, a two-story house with an adjacent kitchen and smokehouse. The university has used this house for many purposes. It was restored, and since 1961 serves as the state headquarters of the Garden Club of Georgia. This beautiful garden is not just a living memorial to the founders, it is also a living laboratory for students of botany, landscape architecture, and ornamental horticulture. Moreover, it's a quiet place to relax and escape the hustle and bustle of a busy campus.

This mature garden features several formal as well as informal sections. The **Formal Boxwood Garden,** with its circular clipped hedges and brick pathways, is surrounded by a white picket fence. Enjoy the **Terrace Garden,** the **Perennial Garden,** and the plantings in two courtyards. Follow the pathways from one garden to the next. Walk through the **Arboretum** or sit quietly on the bench and admire the surrounding beauty. During our spring visit the colors of **azaleas** and **flowering trees** were just spectacular. And our subsequent visit there was almost even more enjoyable. It was late in the day, the sun was beginning to set, the garden was unusually quiet and the heavy fragrance of **cape jasmine** (*Gardenia jasminoides*) was permeating the air. With plantings providing seasonal colors and textures, a visit to this beautifully maintained garden can be enjoyable at any time.

Highlands Region

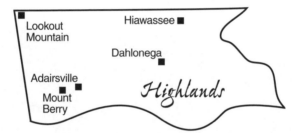

Lookout Mountain

Hiawassee

Dahlonega

Adairsville

Mount Berry

Highlands

Oak Hill and the Martha Berry Museum

Oak Hill is 170 acres of serene beauty. See an 1847 antebellum home, museum, and formal gardens. Enjoy groomed lawns, giant oak trees, and miles of nature trails.

Address: 189 Mount Berry Station, P.O. Box 490189, Mount Berry, GA 30149

Directions: From I-75 take exit 125 and go west on US 441, then connect to GA 20. Continue on GA 20, follow the signs, then connect onto Veterans Memorial Highway (Loop 1). Go north; the entrance will be on your left just before the intersection with US 27.

Hours: 10:00 a.m. to 5:00 p.m Monday to Saturday; 1:00 p.m. to 5:00 p.m. Sunday

Closed: major holidays

Admission fee: yes for museum, grounds free

Wheelchair access: partial

Facilities: gift shop

Area: 170 acres

Phone: (706) 291-1883 or (800) 220-5504

Just outside of Rome and within sight of the Berry College campus lies Oak Hill, a 170-acre plantation and ancestral home of Martha McChesney Berry, founder of Berry College. The mansion, built in 1847 by slave laborers, is a classical Southern plantation house. This design was quite popular in antebellum homes of that time, reflecting the Greek Revival style, with tall ionic columns supporting the front portico. Captain Thomas Berry purchased Oak Hill in 1859 for his bride-to-be, Frances Rhea. Luckily the ravages of the Civil War only very lightly affected Oak Hill. A fire partially damaged just the back portion of the house. This damage was immediately repaired. Captain Berry pledged to settle his debts to Northern creditors before the Civil War hostilities broke out. Hence, he was able to obtain credit from Northern banks after the war, saving his family from financial ruin.

Martha Berry was born in 1866 as the second oldest of Berry's eight children. She was initially tutored at home by the family's governess, and at the age of sixteen was sent to Edgeworth School in Baltimore. She returned home to nurse her father following his stroke. After his death she spent time abroad traveling and studying. It was the log cabin, constructed in 1873 as the playhouse for the Berrys' children, where Martha's vision of educating mind, heart, and hands started. She began teaching Sunday school, but the cabin soon became too small for the crowds longing to learn. Martha Berry strongly believed that "Every human being, regardless of economic circumstances, has a right to become the best that he or she is capable of becoming."

And she soon started to do something about it. She moved from a small log cabin to a larger abandoned old church in Possum Trot, but even that was not enough. In no time she had four Sunday schools and four day schools in the area. She followed her vision and worked tirelessly to make it a reality: from a small boarding school that opened in 1902, to a junior college opened in 1926, to a four-year college with the first graduating class receiving their diplomas in 1932. What a vision, what a story: From humble beginnings in a log cabin originally on eighty-three acres to today's Berry College, one of the premier small colleges in this country, with a campus of twenty-six thousand acres, one of the largest in the world.

Gardens of Oak Hill were opened to the public in 1972. One finds a stroll around Oak Hill very peaceful and serene. As you walk over groomed lawns you feel that majestic **oaks** exude an additional sense of permanence. **Formal Garden** was one of the first gardens planted here in the early 1860s. Flagstone and brick walkways lead through **boxwoods** to a central fountain pool. Annual and seasonal flowers provide an additional accent. The **horseshoe rose garden** that showcases prized hybrid **tea roses** adjoins this area. **Sunken Garden** is a terraced garden with spectacular **Kwanzan cherry trees** that were the official gift of the Japanese government. More than 140 varieties of **daylilies** blossom in this garden as well. **Sundial Garden** features a collection of annuals and perennials. In the **Goldfish Garden,** a traditional knot garden and varieties of annual and perennial plants surround the goldfish pond. Do not miss **Wildflower Meadow** and **Catfish Pond**. There are miles of **nature trails** to explore while enjoying **daffodils, azaleas,** and a multitude of native plants.

Worth seeing:

Visit the **Martha Berry Museum**. Tour begins with viewing of the movie "Miracle in the Mountains." There are many interpretive exhibits chronicling the life of Martha Berry.

Drop in at **Oak Hill**. Martha Berry's family home is beautifully restored and meticulously cared for. It is kept just as it was when she was alive.

Stop by the **Original Cabin,** constructed in 1873 as playhouse for Berry's children. This cabin is known as the "Birthplace of Berry College."

Barnsley Gardens

As you stroll the 30 acres of gardens, you are reminded of ante-
bellum times. A formal boxwood parterre garden, a rose garden,
and native Georgia wildflowers offer beauty as well as a sense of
history.

Address: 597 Barnsley Gardens Road, Adairsville, GA 30103
Directions: From I-75 take exit 128 and go west on GA 140 for
  about 1.5 miles. Follow the signs; there are plenty of them. Make
  a left turn onto Hall Station Road and continue for about 5.5
  miles. Then make a right turn onto Barnsley Gardens Road, and
  after about 2.5 miles the gardens entrance will be on your left.
Hours: Sundays 10:00 a.m. to 4:00 p.m. for public; different hours
  for resort guests
Admission fee: yes
Wheelchair access: partial
Facilities: two restaurants, gift shop, golf, luxurious accommodations
Available: tours by prior appointment
Area: gardens, 30 acres; entire property, 1,200 acres
Phone: (770) 773-7480

Nestled in the rolling hills of northwest Georgia's Bartow
County, just outside of Adairsville and only a few minutes
off busy I-75, Barnsley Gardens combines beauty and
history. There is a certain mystique to the place, believed by many to
have inspired two major books, *Gone With the Wind* and *St. Elmo.* The
history reads just like a storybook. Godfrey Barnsley came to this
country in 1824 from England, just eighteen years old and penniless.
Yet within a few years he became one of the wealthiest cotton
merchants in the South. Over the initial objections of William Scarbrough, principal owner of the *SS Savannah,* the first steamship to
cross the Atlantic Ocean, Barnsley married Scarbrough's daughter,
Julia, in 1828. After a stay in England, the Barnsleys returned to
Savannah. In 1841 the family moved to the mountains of northwest
Georgia, where Godfrey Barnsley started to build Woodlands Manor,
an extravagant estate and family home on 3,500 acres of land for
Julia and their eight children. Julia's unexpected death in 1845 was a
severe blow to Godfrey.

It was probably at this time that he developed his lifelong interest in spiritualism. During his walks through the garden, he claimed he spoke with Julia, who guided him through his efforts to finish the grand twenty-four-room Italian villa manor house. It is believed that the landscape of Woodlands Manor was modeled on published manuals of the premier landscape architect of that time, Andrew Jackson Downing. Godfrey Barnsley introduced hundreds of plants collected from around the world and brought to him by the captains of his ships. These plants were brought to Woodlands Manor, where Godfrey Barnsley continued to direct their plantings in pursuit of his dream. During the Civil War in 1864, Barnsley's estate impressed General James B. McPherson so much that he ordered his occupying Union troops not to damage the property. The soldiers did not damage the estate, but the Civil War eventually did. Godfrey Barnsley believed in the Confederacy. During the war he invested his money in Confederate bonds which became worthless; he even turned his fleet of merchant ships over to the Confederate Navy.

After the war, Godfrey Barnsley made a few unsuccessful attempts to recoup his losses, but to no avail. His fortune was lost, the manor house was left unfinished, and Barnsley died penniless in 1873, just as he had begun, a rags-to-riches-to-rags story. His children inherited the property, and—as if not enough misfortune had happened here—a 1906 tornado left the house in ruins. From here on, the future did not look bright at all. Although the property was listed on the National Register of Historic Places in 1975, its future was still in doubt. And the doubts continued until 1988, when Prince Hubertus Fugger and Princess Alexandra of Germany purchased the estate. They are very much devoted to the preservation of historic structures and started a major restoration project.

As you stroll around, you

cannot help but try to imagine the antebellum times. You simply must admire the formal **Boxwood Parterre Garden** with its central twelve-foot fountain at the front steps of the ruins. Enjoy the **Rose Garden** with over two hundred varieties of roses, including the **green rose**, which is unique to Barnsley Gardens. Marvel over the native Georgia wildflowers blooming in **Wildflower Meadows,** or the colors exploding in the **Perennial Border** that gently surrounds the fallen Confederate colonel's grave. Admire native azaleas in the **Azalea Walk,** and be sure to see **Bog Garden, Lily Pond, Pinetum, Heirloom Orchard,** and **Conifer Collection.**

Antique Rose Emporium

You will see not just roses here. Enjoy the knot garden, the walled garden, the formal perennial border, and even a nature trail.

Address: 5565 Cavender Creek Road, Dahlonega, GA 30533

Directions: From I-285 take exit 19 and go north on GA 400 for about forty-six miles. Go straight through the intersection crossing GA 60 and continue for about 6.5 miles on Long Branch Road. Long Branch Road eventually becomes Copper Mines Road and after about two miles deadends onto Cavender Creek Road. Make a right turn and go on Cavender Creek Road for about a half mile. The entrance to Antique Rose Emporium will be on your left.

Hours: 10:00 a.m. to 5:30 p.m. Tuesday through Saturday; 12:30 p.m. to 5:30 p.m. Sunday

Closed: Easter, July 4th, Thanksgiving, Christmas, and New Year's Day

Admission fee: no

Wheelchair access: yes

Facilities: gift shop, plant nursery

Available: seminars

Area: 2 acres

Phone: (706) 864-5884

Not far from Dahlonega, site of America's gold rush of the 1820s, the Antique Rose Emporium is nicely tucked away in the countryside. Originating in Texas, the Antique Rose Emporium branched into Georgia in 1993. If you fancy old garden roses, this is the place for you.

And to understand this better, let's review the classification of roses. An antique or old garden rose is one that was classified as such prior to 1867; the modern rose is one that belongs to a classification that has evolved since 1867. There are fifteen classes of old garden roses: species, gallica, alba, damask, centifolia, moss, China, tea, noisette, bourbon, hybrid China, hybrid bourbon, hybrid noisette, Portland, and hybrid perpetual. There are ten classes of modern roses: hybrid tea, floribunda, grandiflora, miniature, polyantha,

climbing, shrub, hybrid musk, eglantine hybrids, and rugosa hybrids. There seems to be a resurgence of old garden roses. Modern hybrids were developed for their showy blossoms, and they usually require long hours of fertilizing, spraying, and general care to grow properly. In contrast, old rose varieties do quite well with a minimum of care; some even seem to thrive on neglect as attested to by some beautiful specimens found on abandoned homesites and old cemeteries.

As you stroll around, you see roses everywhere, but it's not just roses. Enjoy walking the paths of the **Display Garden** surrounded by the fragrances and scents of roses, herbs, and perennials. See the **Rose-covered Walkway, Formal Perennial Border, Knot Garden,** and **Walled Garden**. Plantings of a variety of annuals further accentuate the color experience. And if you want to explore more, take the **Nature Trail** through the woods by the Chestatee River. **Rhododendrons, dogwoods,** and **mountain laurels** are just spectacular there.

The Antique Rose Emporium offers roses for sale. Their retail display garden sells containerized roses and a variety of other plants. The knowledgeable staff will give you valuable advice or even identify the rose you brought from home should you be uncertain about it.

You'll find beautiful roses and a lovely site in the countryside.

Rock City Gardens

The 14-acre mountaintop gardens are home to more than four hundred native species of plants and wildflowers. And if that is not enough, on a clear day you can see seven states from the top of Lookout Mountain.

Address: 1400 Patten Road, Lookout Mountain, GA 30750
Directions: From I-75 take I-24 and go west. Take exit 178. Watch for and stay on Lookout Mountain ramp. Go for two blocks and make a left turn on Broad Street. Follow the signs for Rock City. It is about a five-mile drive to get up there.
Hours: 8:30 a.m. to sunset daily
Closed: December 25
Admission fee: yes
Wheelchair access: no
Facilities: café, gift shop
Available: group rates, travel packages for families
Area: 14 acres
Phone: (706) 820-2531

From the top of Lookout Mountain you can see seven states on a clear day, and on any day except Christmas you can visit Rock City Gardens on the top of Lookout Mountain. Garnet and Frieda Carter acquired this rocky mountaintop in the early 1920s as part of a land option deal to develop a tract of land on Lookout Mountain that was to be called Fairyland. Frieda and Garnet Carter were essentially opposites of each other. She was quiet, an artist and musician, who enjoyed collecting indigenous plants and transplanting them all over their property, called Rock City. Garnet Carter, on the other hand, was a wheeler-dealer entrepreneur and promoter who was always working several ventures and real estate developments at the same time. And Garnet was certainly smooth. When the construction of a golf course near his luxurious inn took longer than anticipated, he created the first miniature golf course and started to franchise miniature golf courses all over the United States.

When the Great Depression arrived and the real estate boom

fizzled out, Garnet started to look at Frieda's rocky gardens with increasing interest. He visualized rock gardens as an attraction that had a business potential, that people would come and pay to see. And so it happened. On May 21, 1932, the Carters opened their Rock City Gardens to the public. Initially not many tourists flocked to the gardens.

Garnet, always the promoter, realized he had to do something to spread the word and advertise Rock City. In 1935, together with his friend, an owner of an advertising company, they came on an ingenious idea: to advertise on strategically placed barns along the highways. If the farmer would let them paint their message on the roof of the barn, they would paint the barn for free. The rest is history. In the next thirty years more than nine hundred barns from Florida to the Canadian border were painted this way. The three words "See Rock City" became one of the most successful, famous, and recognizable advertising slogans of all time, a bit of true Americana. Today, almost one hundred barns carrying this slogan still survive.

The mountaintop gardens are home to more than four hundred native species of wildflowers, shrubs, and other plants. Enjoy **ferns, azaleas, rhododendrons,** and **mountain laurels.** And yes, on a clear day, from **Lover's Leap,** you can see seven states: Virginia, Tennessee, Kentucky, Georgia, North and South Carolina, and Alabama.

Fred Hamilton Rhododendron Garden

On 17 acres, this is the largest public rhododendron garden in Georgia. More than three thousand plants represent more than four hundred varieties.

Address: P.O. Box 444, Hiawassee, GA 30546

Directions: From I-85 take exit 45 and continue on I-985 until Gainesville. There take exit 6 and continue north on US 129 until Cleveland, and further north on US 75 to Hiawassee. From Hiawassee take US 76 and go west for about one mile. The entrance to the garden and Georgia Mountain Fairgrounds will be on your right.

Hours: Open daily from sunrise to sunset

Admission fee: no

Wheelchair access: partial

Facilities: none

Area: 17 acres

Phone: (706) 896-4191

This largest public rhododendron garden in Georgia is nestled in Towns County, within sight of Brasstown Bald, which is the highest point in Georgia and a stone's throw away from Lake Chatuge.

Fred and Hazel Hamilton's fascination with **rhododendrons** began in the early 1950s. Over the years they gradually enlarged their collection of hybrid rhododendrons until it eventually grew to almost fifteen hundred plants. Friends and neighbors would come and admire their garden, but the Hamiltons wanted to share the beauty of rhododendrons with even more people. They realized that the garden had to be more accessible. In 1982 Hamiltons donated their garden to the Georgia Mountain State Fair. A new site for the garden was selected near Lake Chatuge and more than fifteen hundred rhododendrons were moved and planted in this new location. The first **Rhododendron Festival** was held in the garden in 1990, and since that time it has become an annual event. The rhododendron collection is continually growing. Many more plants were donated by the Hamiltons or added by the Georgia Mountain State Fair. At the present time there are more than three thousand plants, representing more than four hundred varieties.

Gardeners certainly distinguish between azaleas and rhododendrons. And from a horticultural point of view, azaleas are grouped separately since they are differentiated fairly easily from cultivated rhododendrons. Also, their landscaping uses and growth requirements are somewhat different. Usually azaleas have funnel-shaped, solitary flowers that have five stamens each and fairly small leaves. By contrast, rhododendrons have bell-shaped flowers that have ten or more stamens and large leaves. If it were only that simple. As more species became described, multitudes of exceptions emerged and many differences vanished.

There are about eight hundred species of rhododendrons, and their hybrids are too numerous to count. But keep in mind that botanically speaking, all azaleas and rhododendrons are in the genus *Rhododendron.*

As you stroll along the pine-bark trail you will see rhododendrons everywhere, but you will also enjoy **dogwoods, native azaleas,** and **tulip magnolias**. Mature hardwoods provide pleasant shade. Feast your eyes on **trilliums, lady's slippers,** and a wide variety of other native **wildflowers**. This garden is very tranquil and relaxing.

Other Places of Interest to Garden and Plant Lovers

Highlands Region

Black's Bluff Preserve
Black's Bluff Road
Rome, GA 30161
(404) 873-6946
Owned by The Nature Conservancy, this 107-acre preserve has a rich oak-hickory forest along the Coosa River, an area long regarded by naturalists as one of the most botanically diverse areas of Georgia. The walking trail will lead you through the preserve. Please contact The Nature Conservancy of Georgia at the above telephone number prior to your visit.

Cloudland Canyon State Park
122 Cloudland Canyon Park Road
Rising Fawn, GA 30738
(706) 657-4050
This is one of the most scenic parks in the state, located on the western edge of Lookout Mountain. The park encompasses 2,219 acres, and the scenery is just spectacular. Don't miss the Wild-flower Program in April.

Elachee Nature Science Center
2125 Elachee Drive
Gainesville, GA 30504
(770) 535-1976
A 1,200-acre nature center where emphasis is placed on educating the public about nature. Featured are three nature trails, Wildlife Garden and Trail, and a museum. The center also houses exhibits and classrooms.

Gardens de Pajarito Montana
(Gardens of Little Bird Mountain)
Rt. 4, Box 1181
Canton, GA 30114
(404) 479-4471
The thirty-acre private garden, part of the old Byrd Plantation, is devoted to the study and conservation of native plants, with sections for foreign and exotic species as well.
This is a private garden, visitors by appointment only.

Marshall Forest Preserve
Horseleg Creek Road
Rome, GA 30161
(404) 873-6946
This 293-acre preserve was named Georgia's first National Natural Landmark in 1966 and is now owned by The Nature Conservancy. Once belonging to the Cherokee nation, it is one of the few remaining old-growth forests, supporting more than three hundred species of plants. There are three distinct plant communities: chestnut-oak, pine-oak, and mixed hardwood forest, which contain more than fifty-five species of trees. The preserve also contains the largest population in Georgia of the endangered large-flowered skullcap. Enjoy the nature trails. Flower Glen Trail, named for the numerous, gorgeous flowers blooming here during the spring and summer, extends about a quarter mile into the last old-growth forest in northwest Georgia. There is also a walking trail for the visually impaired, known as the Big Pine Braille Trail. Please contact The Nature Conservancy of Georgia at the above telephone number prior to your visit.

Smithgall Woods–Dukes Creek Conservation Area
61 Tsalaki Trail
Helen, GA 30545
(706) 878-3087
Explore along nature trails or just observe wildlife among the 5,562 acres. Guided tours and educational programs are available.

Tallulah Gorge State Park
P.O. Box 248
Tallulah Falls, GA 30573
(706) 754-7970
This park features one of the most spectacular gorges in the eastern United States. The chasm is two miles long and almost a thousand feet deep. There are several miles of trails.

Vogel State Park
7485 Vogel State Park Road
Blairsville, GA 30512
(706) 745-2628
Located at the base of Blood Mountain in the Chattahoochee National Forest is one of Georgia's oldest and most popular state parks. This 280-acre park surrounds a 20-acre lake, and there are miles of trails. Enjoy the Wildflower Program in the spring, or the color transformation of the Blue Ridge Mountains in the fall.

Piedmont Region

A. H. Stephens State Historic Park
P.O. Box 283
Crawfordville, GA 30631
(706) 456-2602
This is a beautiful, 1,200-acre park for both nature lovers and history buffs, with nature trails and educational and interpretive programs. A Confederate museum houses one of the finest collections of Civil War artifacts in the state of Georgia.

Antebellum Plantation
Stone Mountain Park
P.O. Box 778
Stone Mountain, GA 30086
(770) 498-5690 or (800) 317-2006
A visit here will provide you with a realistic portrayal of life on a pre–Civil War Georgia plantation. The collection of nineteen houses includes original buildings, constructed between 1790 and 1845 and chosen for their authenticity and historical value. They were moved to Stone Mountain Park from their original locations, carefully reassembled and painstakingly restored. Do not miss the recreated boxwood garden at Thornton House, the kitchen garden by the cookhouse, and Formal Garden with gazebo adjacent to Dickey House.

Callanwolde Fine Arts Center
980 Briarcliff Road NE
Atlanta, GA 30306
(404) 872-5338
Built in 1920 by Charles H. Candler, the eldest son of Asa Candler, founder of Coca-Cola, this Gothic-Tudor, 27,000-square-foot mansion is surrounded by twelve acres of lush grounds. There is a rock garden as well as nature trails. The conservatory serves as headquarters for the DeKalb County Federation of Garden Clubs. The center offers classes, workshops, exhibits, concerts, and special events.

Chattahoochee Nature Center

9135 Willeo Road
Roswell, GA 30075
(770) 992-2055

This 127-acre site was once the home of Cherokee Indians who were later displaced by white settlers. Now a nature center, it is home to many native plants and a great variety of wildlife. The center features Woodland Nature Trail, Wildflower Trail, and a boardwalk winding its way through marshlands. Enjoy Fern Garden, Native Plants Garden, and Bog Garden. Birds of Prey Aviary features raptors indigenous to this area that because of their injuries cannot be released back into the wild.

Cochran Mill Nature Center and Arboretum

P.O. Box 911
Fairburn, GA 30213
(770) 306-0914

Opened to the public in 1994, this fifty-acre, privately owned nature center and arboretum is dedicated to educating the public about our environmental responsibilities. There are nature trails and ruins of the old gristmill.

Dauset Trails Nature Center

360 Mount Vernon Church Road
Jackson, GA 30233
(770) 775-6798

More than six miles of nature trails are featured in this 1,100-acre center. Enjoy wildflowers, birds, and all sorts of wildlife. The center offers a multitude of environmental education programs.

Dunwoody Nature Center

5343 Roberts Drive
Dunwoody, GA 30338
(770) 394-3322

The twelve-acre nature center was established for the purpose of improving, developing, and preserving DeKalb County's Dunwoody Park. The nature trail takes visitors through the various habitats of this area: a hardwood and pine forest, a meadow, a wetland, and a Piedmont creek. A major highlight for children and adults alike are the thirteen talking trees strategically placed along the trail.

Fort Yargo State Park
P. O. Box 764
Winder, GA 30680
(770) 867-3489
This 1,850-acre historical park features one of the four log forts or blockhouses built in 1792 by settlers for protection against Cherokee and Creek Indians. Visit the Interpretive Center and explore nature and hiking trails.

Governor's Mansion Gardens
391 West Paces Ferry Road, NW
Atlanta, GA 30305
(404) 261-1776
The mansion, designed in the Greek Revival style, contains thirty rooms totaling 24,000 square feet and is located on eighteen acres of wooded grounds. The mansion's interior can be seen Tuesdays through Thursdays 10:00 a.m. to 11:30 a.m. Although for security reasons you cannot wander through the gardens, most of the gardens can be viewed from the veranda of the mansion. Spring is probably the best time to be here, since the blossoms of azaleas, dogwoods, and cherry trees are just spectacular. Thousands upon thousands of bulbs and spring and summer annuals add quite remarkable colors as well.

Hamburg State Park
Route 1, Box 233
Mitchell, GA 30820
(912) 552-2393
This is a 750-acre park, with a 225-acre lake and nature trail. See the museum and water-powered grist mill still operating today. Inquire about educational programs.

Meadow Garden
1320 Independence Drive
Augusta, GA 30901
(706) 724-4174

Meadow Garden, near the Augusta Canal, is the former home of George Walton, a signer of the Declaration of Independence, member of the second Continental Congress, Chief Justice of Georgia, twice governor of Georgia, and a U.S. senator. Enjoy the grounds surrounding this historic house, which is a National Historic Landmark.

Melvin L. Newman Wetlands Center
2755 Freeman Road
Hampton, GA 30228
(770) 603-5606
This thirty-two-acre center demonstrates the importance of preserving the wetland environment. Explore along Wetland Trail and Boardwalk.

Mistletoe State Park
3723 Mistletoe Road
Appling, GA 30802
(706) 541-0321
A 1,920-acre park, and a 70,000-acre lake—can you imagine that? The park offers nature trails, wildlife observation area, birding, and more.

Panola Mountain State Conservation Park
2600 Highway 155, SW
Stockbridge, GA 30281
(770) 389-7801
Established in 1971 as Georgia's first conservation park and created to protect a 100-acre granite mountain, the park presently includes 633 acres. Essentially untouched by humans, Panola Mountain shelters rare plants and animals of this region. The mountain provides spectacular views of surrounding areas. Follow self-guided trails through the forests of hardwoods and pines or join park staff for a guided hike into the conservation area. There is also an interpretive center and 3.5-mile guided trail. A variety of programs are offered, including wildflower walks in the spring and fall.

Piedmont Park
Piedmont Avenue at 12th Avenue
Atlanta, GA 30306
(404) 658-6116
This 180-acre park was originally the site of the 1895 Cotton
States Exposition. Noted landscape architect Frederick Law
Olmsted was originally consulted on the park's design, but his
ideas were not utilized. However, in 1909 his sons, the Olmsted
brothers, submitted a design which was accepted.

Richard B. Russell State Park
2650 Russell State Park Road
Elberton, GA 30635
(706) 213-2045
The 2,700-acre park is adjacent to a 26,500-acre lake. Explore
the 2.2-mile nature trail through the woods and along the lake
shoreline to one of the oldest steel pin bridges in the area.

Riverwalk
Augusta/Richmond County Convention and Visitors Bureau
P.O. Box 1331
Augusta, GA 30903
(706) 823-6600
Visiting Augusta—especially in the spring—you immediately
understand why it is also called "Garden City." Riverwalk
encompasses five city blocks along the Savannah River. There are
two beautifully landscaped promenades, one at the top of the
levee and the second just above the riverbank. Also featured is
the Japanese Garden, a gift to Augusta from the people of Japan.
Views of the city and the river from the top promenade are just
breathtaking.

Sandy Creek Nature Center
205 Old Commerce Road
Athens, GA 30607
(706) 613-3615
The Center encompasses 225 acres. Well-marked, self-guided
trails wind through the various habitats typical of the Piedmont
region. Brochures with trail maps are available; also featured is
an interpretive center.

Taylor-Grady House
634 Prince Avenue
Athens, GA 30601
(706) 549-8688
Taylor-Grady House is a Greek Revival mansion built in the
1840s by General Robert Taylor, a cotton planter and merchant.
In 1863 the family of Henry W. Grady, who became managing
editor of the *Atlanta Constitution,* purchased the mansion. A great
orator and considered by many to be the spokesman of the New
South, Grady stressed the importance of reconciliation between
the North and South following the Civil War. The house was
restored and furnished in period style and designated as a
National Historic Landmark in 1976. Enjoy beautiful grounds
surrounding this mansion.

Watson Mill Bridge State Park
650 Watson Mill Road
Comer, GA 30629
(706) 783-5349
One of the most picturesque of Georgia's state parks, it encompasses 783 acres and contains the longest covered bridge in
Georgia. Several nature trails allow you to explore the back-
country or the forest along the river.

William H. Reynolds Nature Preserve
5665 Reynolds Road
Morrow, GA 30260
(404) 961-9257
Several trails wind through the woods and wetlands of this 130-
acre preserve. Also featured are the Interpretive Center,
displaying local wildlife in its natural habitat, Heritage
Vegetable Garden, and Herb Garden.

ZOO Atlanta
800 Cherokee Avenue, SE
Atlanta, GA 30306
(404) 624-5600
ZOO Atlanta, open to the public since 1889, is "a private
nonprofit wildlife park and zoological trust empowered to

exhibit, interpret, study, and care for wildlife in superior environments, to conserve biodiversity throughout the world, to educate, enlighten and entertain the public and to contribute to the cultural life of the community." They certainly do all that and much more. And during your visit not only the animals, but also the plants, trees, and landscape will amaze you.

Plains Region

Big Oak
Crawford and East Monroe Streets
Thomasville, GA 31792
(912) 226-9600
Quite a landmark, this majestic live oak, over three hundred
years old, reaches 68 feet into the air, and has a 162-foot limb
span and 24-foot trunk circumference.

Birdsong Nature Center
2106 Meridian Road
Thomasville, GA 31792
(912) 377-4408
This was once a working plantation named Birdsong Plantation,
but now it is a nature preserve and wildlife sanctuary. There are
twelve miles of trails, and plantings of native plants provide food
for birds and butterflies. Trail maps and a variety of nature-
oriented programs are offered to the public.

George T. Bagby State Park and Lodge
Route 1, Box 201
Fort Gaines, GA 31751
(912) 768-2571
This three hundred-acre park is located on the shores of a
48,000-acre lake. Look for wildlife along the wildlife trail
winding through hardwoods and pines.

Melhana
301 Showboat Lane
Thomasville, GA 31792
(912) 226-2290
(888) 920-3030
Developed by industrialist Howard Melville Hanna during the
late 1800s, this site, Thomas County's only plantation, is open
for overnight guests. English gardens have been restored to their
original luxury and elegance.

Old Governor's Mansion
120 South Clarke Street
Milledgeville, GA 31061
(912) 445-4545
Milledgeville was Georgia's state capital from 1803 to 1868, and
the Old Governor's Mansion was the home of nine Georgia
governors between 1839 and 1868. It became part of Georgia
College & State University in 1889 and was designated a
National Historic Landmark in 1971. The mansion is furnished
in period antiques and is open for guided tours. The grounds
surrounding this imposing Greek Revival mansion are beautifully kept.

Piedmont National Wildlife Refuge
Route 1, Box 670
Round Oak, GA 31038
(912) 986-5441
This 35,000-acre wildlife refuge serves as a model of forest
ecosystem management. The forests are of predominantly loblolly
pine. There are many diverse plant habitats for nearly two
hundred species of birds, including the endangered red-cockaded
woodpecker.

Providence Canyon State Conservation Park
Route 1, Box 158
Lumpkin, GA 31815
(912) 838-6202
Wonder at the amazing hues and colors of Georgia's "Little
Grand Canyon." Enjoy the multitude of wildflowers as well as
rare plumleaf azalea. There is an interpretive center.

Reed Bingham State Park
Box 394 B-1, Route 2
Adel, GA 31620
(912) 896-3551
This 1,620-acre park surrounds a 375-acre lake. Walk along the
Coastal Plains Nature Trail that will lead you through a cypress
swamp, pitcher plant bog, sandhill areas, as well as other plant
habitats representative of this region of southern Georgia.

Observe the waterfowl and follow the half-mile Gopher Tortoise Nature Trail. Both the gopher tortoise and the indigo snake are threatened species; you will see plenty of other creatures as well.

Seminole State Park
Route 2
Donalsonville, GA 31745
(912) 861-3137
This 343-acre park sits on beautiful 37,500-acre Lake Seminole. The threatened gopher tortoise, which is the only tortoise native to Georgia, can be seen along the two-mile nature trail designed to interpret the wiregrass community habitat.

Sidney Lanier Cottage
935 High Street
Macon, GA 31201
(912) 743-3851
Birthplace of the great American poet Sidney Clopton Lanier, who was born here in the home of his grandparents in 1842. The park in front of the house is named for him, and live oaks there are reminiscent of his poem "The Marshes of Glynn." A small boxwood garden is behind the house.

Westville Living History Village
Dr. Martin Luther King Jr. Drive
Lumpkin, GA 31815
(912) 838-6310
Westville is a living history village of thirty-two relocated and restored buildings portraying 1850s life in Georgia. There is plenty to see and learn, from a doctor's office, mansion, blacksmith and potter's shop, to a farm complex with cotton gin and cotton bailing press. Costumed craftsmen demonstrate their skills, and you can watch how tools, pottery, quilts, shoes, soap, and candles used to be made.

Coastal Region

Crooked River State Park
3092 Spur 40
St. Marys, GA 31558
(912) 882-5256
This five-hundred-acre park is located on the south bank of the Crooked River in a beautiful coastal setting. Featured are a 1.5-mile nature trail and ruins of the tabby McIntosh Sugar Works mill, built around 1825 and used as a starch factory during the Civil War.

Cumberland Island National Seashore
P. O. Box 806
St. Marys, GA 31558
(912) 882-4336
This 18-mile long and 3-mile wide island parallels Georgia's coast. White sandy beaches on the eastern shore gradually rise to dunes and then give way to a forest of palmettos, pines, magnolias, and oaks. More than three hundred species of birds have been observed here. The only access is by a National Park Service ferry. Since just three hundred visitors are permitted per day, reservations are required.

Forsyth Park
Park and Tree Commission
P. O. Box 1027
Savannah, GA 31401
(912) 651-6610
This twenty-acre park sometimes referred to as Savannah's "Last Square" is named for John Forsyth, governor of Georgia and secretary of state under presidents Andrew Jackson and Martin Van Buren. The park is especially beautiful during spring with its flowering trees and azaleas under the canopy of live oak trees. The park features the Fragrance Garden for the blind, a large fountain dating from 1858, and a memorial commemorating Savannah's Confederate soldiers. The park is on Bull Street, between Gaston Street and Park Avenue.

Fort McAllister State Historic Park
3894 Fort McAllister Road
Richmond Hill, GA 31324
(912) 727-2339 or 727-3614
The 1,690-acre park sits on the south bank of the Great
Ogeechee River. Enjoy giant live oaks and beautiful salt marsh.
And for the history buffs, there is the best-preserved earthwork
fortification of the Confederacy, as well as a museum containing
Civil War artifacts.

General Coffee State Park
46 John Coffee Road
Nicholls, GA 31554
(912) 384-7082
This is a beautiful park on 1,510 acres. Seventeen-Mile River
slowly meanders through a cypress swamp. In this nature
preserve, many of south Georgia's rare and endangered species of
plants can still be seen. Many species of wildlife, including the
threatened indigo snake and gopher tortoise, may be found here
as well. A fifteen-mile nature trail is waiting to be explored.
Agricultural history is interpreted at Heritage Farm. Several
nature and history programs are offered here.

George L. Smith State Park
P. O. Box 57
Twin City, GA 30471
(912) 763-2759
This quiet and secluded park claims 1,638 acres with a 412-acre
lake. Moss-draped cypress trees dot the grist millpond. Walk the
nature trails; white ibis, blue heron, or even threatened gopher
tortoise can be seen here.

Hofwyl-Broadfield Plantation
5556 U.S. Hwy. 17 N
Brunswick, GA 31525
(912) 264-7333
Here you can take a glimpse into early 1800s life on a Georgia
rice plantation. William Brailsford purchased this tract of land in
1806 and named it Broadfield. The present house, built by later

generations of owners in the 1850s, was named Hofwyl. The estate remained in family ownership until 1973. At the present time, the plantation is a 1,268-acre wildlife preserve, showcasing the plant and animal life native to this part of Georgia's fresh-water marsh. Museum exhibits and a videotape presentation show the history of Hofwyl and the rice industry, carved by slaves out of the cypress swamp along the Altamaha River.

Laura S. Walker State Park
5653 Laura Walker Road
Waycross, GA 31503
(912) 287-4900
A 631-acre park is home to several plant communities as well as abundant wildlife. It offers a nature trail.

Little Ocmulgee State Park and Lodge
P. O. Drawer 149
McRae, GA 31055
(912) 868-7474
Featured in the 1,397-acre park are a 265-acre lake, a nature trail, and an interpretive boardwalk.

Magnolia Springs State Park
Route 5, Box 488
Millen, GA 30442
(912) 982-1660
A 948-acre park known for its crystal clear springs that produce an estimated nine million gallons of water daily. The site was used as a prison during the Civil War. Featured are three nature trails, natural spring with interpretive boardwalk, aquarium, and historical exhibits.

Okefenokee National Wildlife Refuge
Route 2, Box 3330
Folkston, GA 31537
(912) 496-7836
This refuge was established in 1937 to preserve the 438,000-acre Okefenokee Swamp. The swamp extends thirty-eight miles north to south and twenty-five miles east to west. To further protect

this unique ecosystem, the interior 396,000 acres of the refuge
were designated a National Wilderness Area. Okefenokee Swamp
is a vast, freshwater bog that was once part of the ocean floor, but
now lies 103 to 128 feet above sea level. Okefenokee means "land
of the trembling earth." Peat deposits many feet thick cover
much of the swamp floor and in spots are so unstable that one
can cause trees and bushes to tremble by stomping the surface.
Okefenokee NWR truly is a mosaic of different habitats, plants,
and wildlife, and it is up to you what you want to enjoy, observe,
or learn. There are nature trails, boardwalks, and interpretive
displays. Guided tours, interpretive programs, and lectures are
available.
Okefenokee National Wildlife Refuge is accessible via three
entrances:

> Eastern or main entrance at Suwannee Canal Recreation Area,
> Folkston, GA (912) 496-7836;
> Western entrance at Stephen C. Foster State Park, Fargo, GA
> (912) 637-5274;
> Northern entrance at the Okefenokee Swamp Park,
> Waycross, GA (912) 283-0583.

Okefenokee Swamp Park
5700 Okefenokee Swamp Park Road
Waycross, GA 31501
(912) 283-0583
Situated on Cowhouse Island, this 1,600-acre wildlife sanctuary
features a wilderness walkway, an observation tower, and flower
gardens. Educational centers offer exhibits about the swamp and
its native birds and animals. At Pioneer Island, accessible by a
boardwalk, an outdoor museum features displays and exhibits
about the early swamp settlers. A variety of swamp animals and
their habitats are featured, such as alligators, turtles, otters, deer,
and turkeys. There are also videotaped shows and live reptile
presentations. The Swamp Creation Center has animated exhibits
and charts explaining the swamp's evolution. The Living Swamp
Ecological Center features a wildlife observation room, an exhibit
of carnivorous plants, a bear observatory, and a serpentarium.
Optional guided boat tours offering a closer look at the wildlife
and plants of the swamp are available.

Sapelo Island National Estuarine Research Reserve
P. O. Box 15
Sapelo Island, GA 31327
(912) 485-2251
Sapelo Island is rich in natural as well as cultural history. The reserve covers 6,110 acres, and visitors can observe the diverse natural communities of a barrier island: from beach and dune systems, to salt marsh and the forested uplands. Observe birds or wildlife, walk the nature trail, or take a guided tour.

Savannah Coastal National Wildlife Refuges
Parkway Business Center, Suite 10
1000 Business Center Drive
Savannah, GA 31405
(912) 652-4415
The seven national wildlife refuges stretch over one hundred miles of coastline and cover over 53,340 acres.
- Pickney Island NWR encompasses 4,053 acres of salt marshes, freshwater ponds, fallow fields, brushland, and forest habitats that support a diversity of plant and bird life. Over fourteen miles of trails are here to be explored.
- Savannah NWR covers 25,608 acres of freshwater marshes, tidal creeks and rivers, and bottomland hardwoods such as cypress, gum, and maple. Most of the freshwater ponds now managed for migratory waterfowl were originally rice fields of plantations. Opportunities to watch birds and alligators abound.
- Tybee NWR, located in the mouth of the Savannah River, provides a resting and feeding place for several species of migratory birds. This refuge is closed to the public.
- Wassaw NWR, located on one of the barrier islands, covers 10,070 acres of salt marshes, beaches, rolling dunes, and woodlands of live oak and slash pine. Follow the trails, and enjoy beachcombing and birdwatching.
- Harris Neck NWR consists of 2,765 acres of saltwater marsh, mixed hardwoods, grasslands, and cropland. These habitats support many species of birds for you to watch, and there are several miles of trails to explore.
- Blackbeard Island NWR covers 5,618 acres of salt and fresh-

water marsh, beach habitat, and maritime forest. Bird-watching here is excellent, and numerous trails and roads provide opportunities for nature study.

- Wolf Island NWR covers 5,126 acres of mostly saltwater marshes with a long narrow strip of beach on the oceanside. The salt water here is open to recreational activities; however, all beach, marsh, and upland are closed to the public.

Savannah Squares
Park and Tree Commission
P.O. Box 1027
Savannah, GA 31401
(912) 651-6610
General James Edward Oglethorpe and 114 colonists arrived at Yamacraw Bluff on the Savannah River on February 12, 1733, to found America's last and thirteenth colony. Within days of his arrival, General Oglethorpe laid out the city of Savannah, making it America's first planned city. It is quite amazing to realize that this was accomplished while the new colony struggled to survive in the New World.

The plan called for rectangular units called wards that were divided into quadrangles. Each quadrangle consisted of a central square, surrounded by trust lots and house lots. Public squares, the integral part of this design, were to be used for open-air markets, social or religious meetings, but also as central areas of fortification. Since Georgia was to act as a buffer between the Spanish-held territory of Florida and the upper twelve colonies.

From 1733 until after the American Revolution, Savannah had only six squares, with Johnson Square being laid out first. By 1851, all twenty-four squares were laid out. Unfortunately two squares were eventually lost. Ellis Square was totally lost, replaced by a garage, and nothing much to mention remains of Liberty Square. But the remaining twenty-two still grace the city today. Beautifully maintained, they provide an oasis of greenery under the shady canopy of stately oaks, a place to sit on a bench to rest or just to admire the surrounding beauty.

You'll find the squares in Savannah's Historic District, recognized as a National Historic Landmark. It covers 2.5 square miles and contains 2,358 buildings of historical significance. The historic district is defined by the Savannah River waterfront to the north, East Broad Street to the east, West Broad Street, now Dr. M. L. King Jr. Boulevard to the west, and Gaston Street to the south. Yes, it is possible to see the squares from the seat of the car. But our advice is—don't do it that way. Get your feet into a comfortable pair of shoes, get a map of Savannah's Historic District in your hand, and you are ready to go. Not only will you be able to see the surrounding beauty first hand, but you will also smell the fresh air and hear the singing of the birds and rustling of the leaves. In almost every block you will find something that is like a page from a history book. You will not regret leaving the car behind.

Squares are presented here from north to south and west to east, rather than in alphabetical order:

Franklin Square, on Montgomery Street (between Bryan and Congress Streets), was laid out in 1790 and named for Benjamin Franklin, American statesman and agent for the colony of Georgia. Part of the square was lost to roadway but the square was partially resurrected; it is now significantly smaller than its original size.

Liberty Square, on Montgomery Street (between State and York Streets), was laid out in 1799 and named to honor the "Sons of Liberty" who fought the British troops during the Revolutionary War. The square was opened to through traffic and the rest was lost to building. There is a marker there that says Liberty Square, but in reality this square no longer exists.

Elbert Square, on Montgomery Street (between Hull and Perry Streets), was laid out in 1801 and named for General Samuel Elbert, a former governor and a member of the Provincial Congress. The square was opened to through traffic, used up for building, and today just a tiny sliver of this square is left.

Ellis Square, on Barnard Street (between Bryan and Congress Streets), was laid out in 1733 and named after Henry Ellis, the second royal governor of Georgia in 1758. The square was the site of the old city market, which was later torn down and replaced by a parking garage in 1954. Today nothing remains of this square.

Telfair Square, on Barnard Street (between State and York Streets), was originally the St. James Square, but renamed for Telfair family in 1883.

Orleans Square, on Barnard Street (between Hull and Perry Streets), honoring the heroes of the War of 1812 Battle of New Orleans, was laid out in 1815.

Pulaski Square, on Barnard Street (between Harris and Charlton Streets), was named for Count Casimir Pulaski, Revolutionary War hero who died during the siege of Savannah in 1779. The square was laid out in 1837.

Chatham Square, on Barnard Street (between Taylor and Gordon Streets), was laid out in 1847 and named after William Pitt, the Earl of Chatham, in 1851.

Johnson Square, on Bull Street (between Bryan and Congress Streets), was the first of the squares laid out. It was named for Robert Johnson, a governor of South Carolina who greatly helped the Georgia colony. In the center of this square are the grave and monument of General Nathaniel Greene.

Wright Square, on Bull Street (between State and York Streets), was named for Sir James Wright, Georgia's third and last colonial governor. The monument in this square honors William Washington Gordon, an early mayor of Savannah. A large boulder marks the grave of Yamacraw Indian chief Tomo-chi-chi, who welcomed General Oglethorpe and the colonists.

Chippewa Square, on Bull Street (between Perry and Hull Streets), was named to commemorate the Battle of Chippewa in Canada in 1814. The bronze statue of General Oglethorpe by Daniel Chester French graces this square.

Madison Square, on Bull Street (between Harris and Charlton Streets), was named in honor of James Madison, the fourth U.S. president. The statue in this square honors Sgt. William Jasper, who was killed in the Siege of Savannah in 1779.

Monterey Square, on Bull Street (between Taylor and Gordon Streets), was named to commemorate the Mexican War Battle of Monterey. However, this square has a monument honoring Count Casimir Pulaski, who died in the Siege of Savannah in 1779.

Reynolds Square, on Abercorn Street (between Bryan and Congress Streets), was named for Captain John Reynolds, governor of Georgia in 1754. The Methodists of Georgia erected the statue of John Wesley in 1969.

Oglethorpe Square, on Abercorn Street (between State and York Streets), was named for General James Edward Oglethorpe, and laid out in 1742.

Lafayette Square, on Abercorn Street (between Harris and Charlton Streets), was laid out in 1837. It was named after the Marquis de Lafayette, who spoke to the people of Savannah from the balcony of the Owens-Thomas house, located on this square, in 1825.

Calhoun Square, on Abercorn Street (between Taylor and Gordon Streets), was laid out in 1851 and named for South Carolina statesman, John C. Calhoun.

Warren Square, on Habersham Street (between Bryan and Congress Streets), was laid out in 1791 and named for General Joseph Warren, president of the Third Provincial Congress.

Columbia Square, on Habersham Street (between York and State Streets), has a fountain from Wormsloe as its centerpiece.

Troup Square, on Habersham Street (between Harris and Charlton Streets), was named for the Georgia governor George Michael Troup, and laid out in 1851.

Whitefield Square, on Habersham Street (between Gordon and Taylor Streets), was laid out in 1851 and named for George Whitefield, Savannah minister and founder of Bethesda orphanage.

Washington Square, on Houston Street (between Bryan and Congress Streets), was named for General George Washington and laid out in 1790.

Greene Square, on Houston Street (between York and State Streets), named for Revolutionary War General Nathaniel Greene.

Crawford Square, on Houston Street (between Hull and Perry Streets), was laid out in 1841 and named for former governor and U.S. senator, William Harris Crawford.

Skidaway Island State Park
52 Diamond Causeway
Savannah, GA 31411
(912) 598-2300 or (912) 598-2301
This barrier island, located near historic Savannah, has both salt and fresh water due to estuaries and marshes flowing through this area. Two nature trails meander through marshes, long leaf pines, live oaks, and cabbage palmettos. Plenty of wildlife can be observed from trails or observation towers.

Stephen C. Foster State Park
Route 1, Box 131
Fargo, GA 31631
(912) 637-5274
This eighty-acre park is one of the primary entrances to the Okefenokee Swamp. Visit the park Interpretive Center and Museum and then walk the one-mile Trembling Earth Nature Trail, marveling on moss-draped cypress trees rising out the black swamp waters. More than 220 species of birds, 60 species of amphibians, 50 species of reptiles, and 40 species of mammals can be seen here. Guided boat tours are available. Inquire about educational programs.

The Cloister
Sea Island, GA 31561
(800) 732-4752
The grounds of the famous Cloister Hotel (designed by Addison Mizner) feature an exquisite garden landscape, much of which can be attributed to T. M. Baumgardner, the famous landscaper of this area. Nearby, admire the magnificent Avenue of Oaks dating from the days of Retreat Plantation, today the site of the Sea Island Golf Club.

Wormsloe State Historic Site
7601 Skidaway Road
Savannah, GA 31406
(912) 353-3023

A renowned avenue of live oaks will lead you to the tabby ruins
of colonial estate Wormsloe. It was built by Noble Jones who
came to Savannah with General James Oglethorpe in 1733 and
received the land grant from the king of England in 1739. The
estate is now owned in part by descendants of the original owner
and in part by the state of Georgia. The famous allée of live oaks
was started in early 1890s when more than four hundred trees
were planted. And today, 1.5 miles long and 70 feet wide, it is
one of the most impressive avenues of oaks to be found anywhere.
An interpretive nature trail will lead you to the tabby ruins,
Jones family cemetery, and Colonial Life Demonstration Area. In
the interpretive museum visitors can view a film about the
founding of the thirteenth colony as well as artifacts excavated at
Wormsloe.

Where to See Specific Types of Flora

Note: This listing only includes gardens with major displays.

Azaleas:	Callaway Gardens
	Lockerly Arboretum
	State Botanical Garden of Georgia
Bamboo:	Coastal Gardens
Bromeliads:	Atlanta Botanical Garden
	State Botanical Garden of Georgia
Cacti & Succulents:	Atlanta Botanical Garden
Camellias:	Massee Lane Gardens
	Lockerly Arboretum
	Georgia Southern Botanical Garden
Carnivorous plants:	Atlanta Botanical Garden
Dahlias:	State Botanical Garden of Georgia
Daylilies:	Coastal Gardens
Ferns:	Atlanta Botanical Garden
	State Botanical Garden of Georgia
Flowering trees:	Callaway Gardens
	State Botanical Garden of Georgia
	Atlanta Botanical Garden

Herb Gardens:	Atlanta Botanical Garden
	Lockerly Arboretum
	Coastal Gardens
Irises:	Lockerly Arboretum
	Atlanta Botanical Garden
Japanese Gardens:	Atlanta Botanical Garden
	Massee Lane Gardens
Magnolias:	Callaway Gardens
	Coastal Gardens
Orchids:	Atlanta Botanical Garden
	State Botanical Garden of Georgia
	Callaway Gardens
Rhododendrons:	Fred Hamilton Rhododendron Garden
	Callaway Gardens
	Lockerly Arboretum
	State Botanical Garden of Georgia
	Atlanta History Center
Rose Gardens:	Robert Staton Rose Garden
	Thomasville Rose Garden
	Antique Rose Emporium
	Atlanta Botanical Garden
	State Botanical Garden of Georgia
	Massee Lane Gardens
Vegetable Gardens:	Callaway Gardens
	Coastal Gardens
Vines:	Atlanta Botanical Garden
Water lilies:	Atlanta Botanical Garden
	Lockerly Arboretum

A Calendar of Georgia Garden Events

January

Southern Gardening Symposium
Callaway Gardens
(800) 225-5292 or (800) 282- 8181

Winter Orchid Display
Atlanta Botanical Garden
(404) 876-5859

February

Camellia Festival
Massee Lane Gardens
(912) 967-2358

Southeastern Flower Show
Atlanta Botanical Garden
(404) 876-5859

Camellia Show
Atlanta Botanical Garden
(404) 876-5859

March

Plant Fair, Sale and Show
Callaway Gardens
(800) 225-5292 or (800) 282-8181

Cherry Blossom Festival
Macon
(912) 743-3401

Spring Gardening Seminar
Coastal Gardens
(912) 921-5460

Easter Daffodils
Oak Hill and The Martha Berry Museum
(706) 291-1883 or (800) 220-5504

Daffodil Show
Atlanta Botanical Garden
(404) 876-5859

April

Spring Festival and Plant Sale
Georgia Southern Botanical Garden
(912) 871-1114

Rose Show and Festival
Thomasville Rose Garden
(912) 225-3919 or (800) 704-2350

Dogwood Festival
Atlanta
(404) 892-0538

Flower Show
The Crescent
(912) 244-6747

Bloomin' Azaleas
Oak Hill and The Martha Berry Museum
(706) 291-1883 or (800) 220-5504

Herb Education Day
Atlanta Botanical Garden
(404) 876-5859

May

Rhododendron Festival
Georgia Mountain Fair
(706) 896-4191

Hemerocallis Show
The Crescent
(912) 244-6747

Rose Show and Sale
Atlanta Botanical Garden
(404) 876-5859

Hosta Show
Atlanta Botanical Garden
(404) 876-5859

Bonsai Show
Atlanta Botanical Garden
(404) 876-5859

June

Hemerocallis Show
Atlanta Botanical Garden
(404) 876-5859

July

Day Lilies in the Sunken Garden
Oak Hill and The Martha Berry Museum
(706) 291-1883 or (800) 220-5504

August

Herb Days at Callaway Gardens
Callaway Gardens
(800) 225-5292 or (800) 282-8181

September

Fall Plant Sale
DeKalb College Botanical Gardens
(404) 244-5001

October

Native Plants Symposium
Georgia Southern Botanical Garden
(912) 871-1114

Fall Plant Sale
DeKalb College Botanical Gardens
(404) 244-5001

Fall Plant Sale
State Botanical Garden of Georgia
(706) 542-1244

Open House
Antique Rose Emporium
(706) 864-5884

November

Camellia Show
The Crescent
(912) 244-6747

"Orchidfest"
Atlanta Botanical Garden
(404) 876-5859

December

Festival of Trees
Massee Lane Gardens
(912) 967-2358

Index

Frank A. Smith Rhododendron
    Garden, 72
Fred Hamilton Rhododendron Garden,
    103–104
Fruit, 57–58, 68

G

Galle Native Azalea Garden, 86
Garden
    azalea, 30, 54–55, 86
    bog, 30, 75, 85, 98
    botanical, 29, 35, 66, 81, 82, 84
    butterfly, 41, 50, 57-58, 77
    camellia, 30
    dahlia, 87
    daylily, 33
    formal, 39, 42,46, 90, 93
    herb, 33, 50, 58, 67, 77, 85
    hummingbirds, 77
    iris, 69
    Japanese, 46, 67
    kitchen, 30
    parterre, 16, 19, 20, 25
    perennial, 30, 75, 81, 90
    rhododendron, 72, 86, 103
    rose, 30, 46, 67, 77, 78, 83, 87, 95,
        98
    Southern, 16, 20, 34
    vegetable, 33, 57, 69, 77
Gardens de Pajarito Montana, 106
Garfield, Abram and James, 43
Gazebo, 56, 65, 83
    Victorian rose garden, 41
General Coffee State Park, 119
George L. Smith State Park, 119
George T. Bagby State Park and Lodge,
    115
Georgia, 28, 32
    coastal plain, 35, 36
    native plants, 34
    Southern Botanical Garden, 35–36
    Southern University, 35
Goldfish Garden, 95
Gordon, Sarah and William W., 19
Governor's Mansion Gardens, 110
Grain, 31
Grape arbor, 33
Grass, 32-33

Grassmann, Edward J., 48
Green, Charles, 24
Green-Meldrim House, 24–25
Grotto, 58
Groundcover Collection, 87
Guido
    Dr. Michael A., 34
    Evangelistic Association, Inc., 34
    Gardens, 34
Gwinnett County, 82

H

Hamburg State Park, 110
Hamilton, Fred and Hazel, 103
Hammocksweet azalea, 54
Hanna, Howard Melville, 43
Hardwood, 36, 50, 56
Harrison, Colonel Z.D., 76
Hawthorns, 50
Heirloom Orchard, 98
Hemerocallis, 33
Hemp, 28
Herb, 33, 58, 72, 100
    culinary and fragrance, 50, 58, 67,
        85
    medicinal, 50, 58, 67, 85
    parterre, 30
Heritage Zone, 36
Hiawassee, 103
Highlands Region, 91–104
Historic Savannah Foundation, 17, 26
Hjort, Peter J., 41
Hofwyl-Broadfield Plantation, 119
Home Demonstration Garden, 58
Hostas, 50, 83
Hummingbirds, 16, 58, 77, 87

I

Ida Cason Callaway Memorial Chapel,
    55–56, 59
Indigo, 28
Ireland, Elizabeth "Pansy," 43
Iris, 50, 81
Isaiah Davenport House Museum,
    17–18

Here are some other books from Pineapple Press on related topics. For a complete catalog, write to Pineapple Press, P.O. Box 3899, Sarasota, Florida 34230-3899, or call (800) 746-3275. Or visit our website at www.pineapplepress.com.

Guide to the Gardens of Florida by Lilly Pinkas. Organized by region, this guide provides detailed information about the featured species and facilities offered by Florida's public gardens. Includes 16 pages of color photos and 40 line drawings.

Seashore Plants of South Florida and the Caribbean by David W. Nellis. A full-color guide to the flora of seashore environments, including complete characteristics of each plant as well as ornamental, medicinal, ecological, and other aspects. Suitable for backyard gardeners and serious naturalists.

Georgia's Lighthouses and Historic Coastal Sites by Kevin M. McCarthy. Illustrated by William L. Trotter Here are stories of Civil War soldiers, pioneers and settlers, Native Americans, seafarers and pirates, and even a ghost or two.

Growing Family Fruit and Nut Trees and *Growing and Using Exotic Foods* by Marian Van Atta. How to enjoy all phases of growing your own delicious fruits, nuts, vegetables, herbs, and wild edibles. Includes planting and growing instructions as well as recipes for enjoying your bountiful crops.

Fragrant Flowers of the South by Eve Miranda. Eighty species of blooming plants that will provide fragrance and beauty to any Southern garden. Each species is illustrated by a color photograph or watercolor painting, and each entry discusses uses, hardiness, blooming season, and planting instructions.

Flowering Trees of Florida by Mark Stebbins. If you just can't get enough of majestic trees, brightly colored flowers, and anything that grows from the ground up, you'll love this book. Written for both the seasoned arborist and the weekend gardener alike, this comprehensive guide offers 74 outstanding tropical flowering trees that will grow in Florida's subtropical climate.

The Trees of Florida by Gil Nelson. The first comprehensive guide to Florida's amazing variety of tree species, this book serves as both a reference and a field guide to the naturalist, professional botanist, landscape architect, and weekend gardener.

The Shrubs and Woody Vines of Florida by Gil Nelson. A companion to *The Trees of Florida*, this reference and field guide covers over 550 species of native and naturalized woody shrubs and vines.

The Art of South Florida Gardening by Harold Songdahl and Coralee Leon. Gardening advice specifically written for the unique conditions of south Florida. A practical, comprehensive guide written with humor and know-how.

Landscaping in Florida by Mac Perry. A photo idea book packed with irresistible ideas for inviting entryways, patios, pools, walkways, and more. Over 200 photos and eight pages of color photos, plus charts of plant materials by region, condition of soil and sunlight, and purpose.